The Other Half
of Old New Orleans

The

Collected and Edited by

Published by

OTHER HALF

of

Old New Orleans

Sketches of Characters and Incidents
from the Recorder's Court of New
Orleans in the Eighteen Forties as
Reported in the "Picayune."

E. MERTON COULTER

Professor of History at the University of Georgia

LOUISIANA STATE UNIVERSITY PRESS

To
Wendell Holmes
Stephenson

⟋CONTENTS

INTRODUCTION

New Orleans in 1840 was a vast city, as measured by the standards of those days. Here lived a hundred thousand people who were proud of the fact that their presence made the Crescent City, strung along the banks of the Mississippi, the fourth in size in the Union. The wanderlust which led myriads of Americans to migrate to the West also led many others to this magic, growing city. Some came to make their fortunes and enjoy that wealth which helped so much to add a sort of exotic glamor to life here; others with no substantial means drifted here with a fervor for its sinful attractions as great as that which leads a good Mussulman to see sacred Mecca.

By this time the city had developed a reputation for wickedness equal to that of Sodom and Gomorrah. It was pointed to by the frontier preacher to adorn a sermon, but longed for in every community by the young hot-bloods who felt there was more in life than they were getting. In the famous sermon "Where the Lion Roareth and the Wang-Doodle Mourneth," the Hard-Shell Baptist preacher shouted forth this warning and confession: "Now, 'whar the lion roareth and the wang-doodle mourneth for his first-born'—ah! This part of my tex, my beseaching brethering, is not to be taken as it says. It don't mean the howling wilderness, whar John the Hard-Shell Baptist fed on locusts and wild asses, but it means, my brethering, the city of New Y'Orleans, the mother of harlots and hard lots, whar corn is wuth six bits a bushel one day and nary a red the nex; whar niggers are as thick as black bugs in spiled bacon ham, and gamblers, thieves, and pickpockets goes skiting about the streets like weasels in a barn-yard; whar honest men are scarcer than hen's teeth; and whar a strange woman once took in your beluved teacher, and bamboozled him out of two hundred and twenty-seven dollars in the twinkling of a sheep's-tail; but she *can't* do it again! Hallelujah—ah! 'For they shall gnaw a file, and flee unto the mountains of Hepsidam, whar the lion roareth and the wang-doodle mourneth for his first-born'—ah!" [1]

The ends of the earth had come together to make up this great city. Basically French, it was hard pressed by the coming Americans; but color aplenty was fast being added by the influx of the Irish, the English, and the Scotch, by the Germans, the Dutchmen, the Spaniards, and the Italians. But the river front and the streets gave greatest evidence of the presence of the

---

[1] Quoted in F. J. Meine, ed., *Tall Tales of the Southwest* (New York, 1930), 254–55. By permission of the publisher, Alfred A. Knopf, Inc.

5,000 or 6,000 migratory boatmen from their 1,500 flatboats lying in the river, and of the sailors from the ships of the seven seas. Then there were the "wharf-rats," who seemed to come from nowhere and end up at the same place, described by a contemporary as "a shrewd, cunning class, who pilfer about the Levee during the day and sleep under or about the wharfs at night," and who were "hard and fiendish in their features, and invariably chew tobacco or smoke worthless segars." [2]

There were many amusements well within the reach of this "other half" of New Orleans. Billiard rooms, gambling houses, and lottery offices were as numerous as the stars in the heavens. To an English visitor in 1830, it appeared that every second house in the French Quarter was busily dispensing one of these forms of entertainment.[3] To control the least responsible part of her population, the city had an ordinance requiring that cannon be fired at eight o'clock in the evening in winter and at nine o'clock in summer, to announce to all sailors, soldiers, and negroes that they must get off the streets. As the sun went down, oil lanterns, hanging on every street corner, were lighted; and then the watchmen came out to reign over the city in the dimness of night. Familiarly known as "Char-

[2] *Picayune* (New Orleans), May 7, 1842.
[3] James Stuart, *Three Years in North America* (New York, 1833), II, 130.

lies," they wandered around in pairs or trios, carrying little lanterns, and followed by dogs to help them find their prey.[4]

Though New Orleans might seem wicked, it was not a dangerous city. Its crimes were not of the enormous kind. An English traveler observed: "On the levee there is a great deal of rudeness, and a great deal of swearing, among the cartmen or carters, and among the persons delivering goods from the vessels and loading them, but, upon the whole, New-Orleans appears to be more orderly, or, at least, a far less disorderly, place than I had expected to find it." [5] And the New Orleans *Picayune* declared: "our New Orleans loafers are not generally vicious fellows, such as the police reports of Philadelphia, New York, Boston, Baltimore, and other *pious* and *orderly* cities exhibit; but on the contrary, they are good-natured, jolly, whole-souled sort of chaps, whose only sin is that of taking a *little* too much of the *crathur*. They are not taken up for assaulting ladies in the streets, for riots in houses of ill-fame, for pulling down dwellings and

[4] Much of the atmosphere of old New Orleans may be got not only from the travel books of the day, but also in more accessible but less realistic form from Grace King, *New Orleans, The Place and the People* (New York, 1895), Lyle Saxon, *Fabulous New Orleans* (New York, 1928), and Herbert Asbury, *The French Quarter* (New York, 1936).

[5] Stuart, *Three Years in North America,* II, 132.

setting fire to property, &c. We see these things in the
police reports of other cities, but they are seldom in
our own." [6]

The sketches that make up this volume bear out the
judgment of this New Orleans editor. They are a
selection from the reports of the trials in the Recorder's Court published in the New Orleans *Picayune*
during the years 1840 to 1842.

Who this newspaper reporter was, no one knows
with absolute certainty. There can be no doubt that he
was a person of education, that he was a close observer,
and that he had a sense of humor. What he wrote was
well up to the standards of literary merit which char-
acterized the humorous writers of the Old Southwest
at this time. He had imagination and he never failed
to take full advantage of his opportunities to describe
the scenes and characters incident to the holding of the
Recorder's Court. He declared: "We look out for a
'character' with as much anxiety, almost, but not quite,
as a merchant looks out for his ships at sea—as a stock
jobber looks out for a fall or a rise in the funds—as an
old maid looks out for some one to 'pop the question,'
or as a political editor looks out for 'glorious victo-
ries.' " [7]

The reporter gave considerable rein to his imagina-

[6] August 7, 1840.
[7] *Picayune,* October 3, 1840.

tion in recording conversations and descriptions of scenes which preceded trials in court; but whether true in actual detail or not, his reports gave an accurate picture of the times. These sketches, then, are not only humorous and amusing, but they are valuable as historical documents, descriptive of a numerous element in the surging, the glamorous, the fabulous New Orleans.

There is good reason to believe that George W. Kendall was the author of these sketches. Kendall and Francis Lumsden had set up the New Orleans *Picayune* in January, 1837, and like the editors of those times, they did most of their reporting. Lumsden's characteristics do not suggest him as the reporter for the Recorder's Court; but what is known of Kendall almost unmistakably points to him. He was famous for his wit and his humorous descriptions. In one of his sketches the reporter incidentally stated that he was unmarried; Kendall was a bachelor at this time. Throughout most of 1841, Kendall was absent from New Orleans, having gone with the Texans on the ill-fated Santa Fe expedition; [8] during this time the *Picayune* almost ceased to publish the proceedings of the Recorder's Court, and those published were short

[8] The Republic of Texas, claiming that the Rio Grande was her western boundary, sought to take Santa Fe and establish her jurisdiction in what is now eastern New Mexico. Kendall wrote a history of this expedition: *Narrative of the Santa Fé Expedition.* . . . (New York: Harper & Brothers, 1844. 2 vols.)

reports which could have been written by almost any-
one.

What of the Recorder, whose court afforded so
much grist for the *Picayune*'s mill? His name was
Joshua Baldwin, and he must have been the type of
judge, with his great store of common sense, which
one might still meet on the bench of Old Bailey in
London. New Orleans had been divided into three
municipalities, each with its own city government.
Baldwin dispensed justice in the first instance for the
Second Municipality—the part of the city built up by
the Americans. With all the milk of human kindness
which he must have had in his heart, Baldwin, in
serving many years as Recorder, could not have
hoped to avoid harsh criticism from some of those
who had received justice at his hands, or to escape
actual violence. Once, as he was returning in his gig
from Lake Pontchartrain, he was beset by a gang of
three, stabbed, and robbed of $30 [9]; and once the
editor of the *Picayune* defended him against those
who criticized him for being too rigorous in his judg-
ments: "We always ascribe his conduct in such in-
stances to what he conceived to be a sense of public
duty, and not to an inherent spirit of persecution or
any want of sympathy for the more unfortunate of
his species." [10]

[9] *Picayune,* August 5, 1838.
[10] *Ibid.,* February 19, 1842.

These sketches have been reproduced just as they appeared in the *Picayune*, except for obvious errors of the printers. The titles are mine.

E. M. COULTER

Athens, Georgia
August, 1938

I

Moses A. Trash was yesterday in-
ducted to a seat in the prisoners'
box by one of the police officers. Moses looked like a
man against whom misfortune had been blowing a
hard wind all his life time; his flag of distress seemed
never to have been taken in. He was indeed a ragocrat
legitimately and of right.—"The vorld," said Moses,
as he wended his way up Magazine street about twelve
o'clock on Wednesday night,—"The vorld is a wicious

Humbug

9

vicked vorld and hain't got no sympathy for no one.
If a fellow vishes to rise in an honest vay, the ladder is
pulled from under his feet 'fore he gets up two steps,
and down he comes. If he tries to go ahead on vot's
called equitable principles, he runs off the track in a
short time I tell you. I've rewolved the thing over in
my mind; I looked at it every vhich vay and find it
ain't to be done but by gammon [1]—gammon is a far
better article than anthracite coal for firing up and
keeping on steam if you vant to keep on the railroad
of fortune. I have a scheme now in my mind—'a
grand scheme'—and if that dont succeed I'll report
myself at vonce unfit for service—but it vill, it must,
I know it must; and other fellows vill have a *chance*
of making a fortune right off as vell as I vill."

"I say, mister, vot you mean by placing your thumb
on your nose and vorking your fingers?" asked Moses
of some imaginary, or at least imperceptible person.
"Don't you think it's true; vell I'm blowed if you
don't see it in the papers. Yes, I'll adwertise some real
estate vhich, if I don't own I should own; and the
'fortunate holders' shall be *told* of all kinds of prizes.
Tickets vill be sold off cheap and it vill be a 'rare
chance' for making an inwestment. Vhat's that you
say? (Speaking again to the invisible gentleman,) I
dont own no real estate? Vot of it; ain't a vell painted
map prettier any day than real estate? cant I have

[1] A colloquial expression for humbug.

theatres, hotels and all that sort of things drawn out
on a piece of parchment and made to look just as
nat'ral as life; and if I can raise the vind to pay the
artist von't it be all right, because then it vill be vot I
calls *unincumbered* property. That's the only vay as
I knows on of making a fortin. It's vonderful how
men suffer dust to be thrown in their eyes ven a lottery is in the case; I attributes it myself to a constitutional veakness in their natur, just like drinking
juleps or any other wice; and I doesn't think it can be
'radicated by the State Legislature either, nor in fact
I aint anxious it should till I dispose of my tickets for
the unseen, unknown, unincumbered, grand humbug,
imaginary, real estate, situated and lying and being,
as the lawyers say, in the extensive, flourishing, pros-
perous, and favorably situated city of Smithville,
vhich is to be the future seat of government of all
America; the starting place of the Columbian and
European steam balloon carriages, and the depot of
the Atlantic and Pacific marine rail roads. There, I'd
like to know who vouldn't buy my lottery tickets vith
such a grand flourish as that in an adwertisement—vy
they'll go off like Colt's repeating rifle; they vill, and
no mistake about it."

Feeling in an ecstasy of delight that he had at length
found out the pleasant art of money catching, a science of which he had been in pursuit all his life but
could never get the hang of it—he commenced cut-

ting up as many capers as a man with the poker, or a drunken Indian.

Charley,[2] with that anxiety which he ever evinces for the safety and well being of the citizens, took Moses up and secured him for the night in the calaboose.

The Recorder [3] on hearing his story yesterday morning, came to the conclusion that he followed no honest occupation for a living, and ordered him to be sent to the calaboose for thirty days. There he will have leisure to arrange his plans for the drawing of his grand real estate lottery scheme.

September 4, 1840

Scotchman IN our last report we wanted a hero; to-day we have as many as would, with proper assistance from the canine invincibles,[4]

---

[2] A watchman was familiarly known as "Charley." The tendency was to make him out somewhat of a simpleton but a highly suspicious fellow with an exaggerated contempt for the hard luck stories of New Orleans' ne'er-do-wells. The watchmen carried little lanterns, like *ignes fatui,* and rattles to signal to one another or to help stop thieves. They numbered about fifty, and generally went in groups of two or three, accompanied by a dog or two. An ordinance in 1825 required them to know how to speak both French and English.

[3] Joshua Baldwin was the recorder at this time. He was for many years an important figure in the administration of justice in the Second Municipality of New Orleans.

[4] This refers to the dogs which the watchmen used in finding and capturing culprits.

defeat the Seminoles.[5] Among them was a brawny "chiel fra the land o' cakes," who answered to the popular name of John Smith. His voice was as musical as a Scotch fiddle, and his nose was as variegated with red and blue spots as a highlander's kilt, and beard as strong as the furze of a thistle.

"Is your name John Smith?" said the Recorder.

"Why, your ooner, folks ca' me so," said the prisoner.

"You were found drunk last night," said the Recorder.

"Lord, mon, it's nae sic a thing. I jost met wi' an auld acquaintance, and we had a drap for auld lang syne," said the prisoner.

"What countryman are you?" said the Recorder.

"Aye, I dinna think it's muckle matter aboot that," said the prisoner. "I'm fra Edinboroo in bonny Scotland, and I wad na care if I was back agin."

"The watchman says you were singing," said the Recorder.

"Aye I might ha' been humming like, Loughaber no more, or some sic a thing, but I wasn't macking noo disturbance."

"Well, I'll let you go this time," said the Recorder, "on paying your jail fees; but if brought up again I will send you down."

---

[5] At this time the United States was waging a war against the Seminoles, in Florida, to induce them to migrate to the West.

"Aye, mon, dear, I am goin' doon fast enough o' my own accord; it has been doon, doon, doon, wi' me since I left the banks o' bonny Doon, and see nae likelihood o' me risin'."

After this brief soliloquy John put on his plaid cap and left the office.

September 8, 1840

Politics THERE was a strong force up before Recorder Baldwin yesterday.

Richard King, James P. Nicks and William Harper had a regular set-to—no, a set-*three* fight on the Levee on Monday night. Knock downs were given scientifically, phlebotomy [6] was performed professionally, and gouging done on the latest Kentucky principle.

The three follow the river, at least so they say, and yet they are oftener seen floating up the river than the Benton mint drops.[7] About the proper time for taking a horn they never disagree; about the mode of steering a broadhorn they are unanimous; but about politics, more particularly about the merits of Harri-

---

[6] A medical term used to denote the act of opening a vein to let out blood.

[7] A reference to Thomas Hart Benton's hard money. Benton, a senator from Missouri for thirty years, long opposed the issuing of paper money.

son and Van Buren,[8] their opinions were at right angle triangles.

King and Harper were whole-hog hard ciderites; Nicks, solitary and alone, defended Kinderhook [9] cabbage and the Northern man with Southern principles; he assailed the public character of the hero of North Bend [10] with a virulence that would do justice to a small potato politician, whilst his two opponents bared their breasts to meet the shafts directed at Tippecanoe.[11]

The controversy waxed warm, as all political controversies do, till at length the parties, finding the force of argument insufficient to settle the subject, had recourse to the less philosophical mode of physical force to enforce their opinions.

The battered countenance, bunged-up eyes and bloody nose of Nicks, told plainly that he was in a glorious minority; and but for the interference of the police, Harrison might count with certainty on a negative gain of one at the November elections.

The Recorder having heard with his usual patient

[8] The candidates of the Whig and Democratic parties respectively in the election of 1840.

[9] Van Buren was born in the village of Kinderhook, New York.

[10] Harrison's Ohio home was at this place, a small village on the Ohio River sixteen miles below Cincinnati.

[11] A name applied to Harrison on account of his victory over the Indians at the battle of Tippecanoe, in 1811.

attention the whole case, charge, countercharge and evidence, remanded King and Harper to appear before the Criminal Court for assault and battery, and held Nicks in durance till vouched for.

September 9, 1840

Millerite Fanatic   THE   GREAT   I   AM.—
Among the prisoners who paid their obeisance yesterday to Recorder Baldwin, was Samuel Pointer *alias* "the great I am." Most of our city readers must have recently noticed a man who goes through the highways and byways, preaching about the approaching termination of the world, and proclaiming many other prophetic forebodings. He generally wears a linen, skirted coat, nankeen pants and broad-leafed hat, and does not appear to be so demented as his actions would indicate; his monomania is apparently confined to scriptural revelations.

"Samuel Pointer?" said the Recorder, "Samuel Pointer?"

The Recorder might call spirits from the vast deep, but would they come? and so might he call Samuel Pointer but would he reply? D—d clear of it.

The police officer went over to Pointer, told him to stand up, and asked him why he did not answer [to] his name?

"That," said Pointer, in a sonorous, methodical voice, "That is not my name. *I am the great I am*, and

I have come to tell you of the destruction of the world."

"What does he say?" said the Recorder.

"I say," said Pointer, "that the world was to exist but a time and a time and a half time, and that its dissolution is come. I have been telling this for the last thirty years, and if you be all burned in everlasting fire I'm not to blame."

"Mr. Pointer," said the Recorder, seeming to disregard altogether his admonitions, "you were found lying drunk last night."

"And there appeared another great wonder in heaven," said Pointer, "for behold a great red dragon, having seven heads and ten horns and seven crowns upon his head, appeared to me and related all that is to happen."

"Do you recollect the name of the street in which you were found?" said the Recorder.

"This is the city, sir, that is to be consumed," said Pointer; "you will find it, sir, in the sixteenth chapter and nineteenth verse of Revelations; but I have told it to them over and over again, and they will not believe me. When the fire comes they may cry out, but I will not save one of them. Open the book, sir, and you will find that the great city was divided into three parts,[12] and that the cities of the nation fell."

[12] This is a sly reference to New Orleans, which was divided into three municipalities. The division, which was made in 1831, grew

The Recorder now seemed to have got a clue into
the character he was addressing, and he said—"Mr.
Pointer, I shall let you go this time."

"You—are—right—sir," said Pointer, speaking in
the most measured manner; "because I saw the beasts
and the kings of the earth, and they told me all that
was to happen, for *I am*, sir, *the great I am*—there is
no mistake about it. You know it, sir, and I know it,
and the whole world will know it, for he that sat upon
the throne said unto me, behold I make all things new
—and he said, Write, for these words are true and
faithful. Now, sir, there is no mistake but *I am the
great I am*."

"Take him out!" said the Recorder.

"And he carried me away into the spirit," said
Pointer. Here the watchman took him from the box
and thrust him out of the office just as he was going to
inflict on the court some more of his rambling, uncon-
nected *Millerisms*.[13]

September 12, 1840

out of the rivalry between the French-speaking and English-speaking
parts of the population.

[13] A term applied to the teachings of William Miller, who had
studied deeply the Old Testament prophecies and who came to the
conclusion that Christ would reappear sometime between 1831 and
1844. Miller was born in Pittsfield, Massachusetts, in 1782. He died
in 1849.

THE RECORDER's calendar was not
High
unusually weighty the last two days.
John Wilson was among the number. John is a gone
case, and we believe it would take the almost super-
human powers of a father Mathew to reclaim him.
John's contour of countenance is peculiarly unique,
and we doubt if his portrait could be taken by even a
machine for taking likenesses, which is constructed on
mathematical principles. His forehead was puckered
up like a shut fan; his nose was like one of the fallen-in
wharves of the First Municipality, and seemed to be
attracted by some secret magnetic influence over to his
right ear; his eyes were like two rusty brass nails stuck
in the end of a pedlar's yard stick; his upper lip was
the moulding of a Gothic window; and his teeth were
like petrified marine plants. The course of John as he
navigated along the Levee, was as tortuous as that of
a place-hunting politician.

"I likes to be high," said John, "it's the most happy
time a fellow has. I'd like to be von of them 'ere stars,
'cause then I'd alvays be high, and maybe I vouldn't
shine—eh?—Lor' how I'd vink then at the efforts of
the Charlies to calaboose me. I is a star in my own
sphere, but people haint discovered my genius yet,
and don't patronize me. Ven folks gets over the Elssler [14] fever—vhen the dancin' epidemic dies avay,

[14] Fanny Elssler was a Viennese dancer who came to America in

I'll put forth my pretensions, 'cause I knows I's a star." At this moment Wilson came in contact with a block of logwood which caused him to lose his equilibrium, and the force of gravity brought his body to the ground. "I is a star," repeated John, and—to the logwood—"you is no gentleman to treat me in this here vay." Here he made several spasmodic efforts to rise, but without success.

The watchman came up at the moment and having heard some of the rhapsodies of Wilson, he said—

"Well, you is a star I b'lieve, that's fact, but you is a fallen star."

"You insulted me vithout prowocation," said Wilson—he very naturally mistook Charley for the log of logwood—"and you haint no authority to do no such thing."

"O there's no use in all this here lingo," said Charley; "I sees that your upper works is out of order; we must try if Doctor Baldwin can't prescribe for you. I guess he'll give you a thirty days' dose."

The watchman without more ado took Wilson to the calaboose.

Wilson acknowledged, when questioned by the Recorder, that he did take "a sum'mut" on Saturday night; that what he did to any one or what any one did to him, was all a blank in his memory; that he felt

1840 and set a vogue which became the talk of the country for the next few years.

his head and his shins soreish but could not account for it.

The Recorder indulged in some admirable axioms on the physical, spiritual and temporal advantages to be derived from a life of sobriety; and Wilson having evinced his tacit assent of their truth, he was discharged.

September 15, 1840

Personal Liberty THOMAS CUNNIFF was the first person called up yesterday morning, and he was in no particular hurry in obeying the summons. He looked lazy and loaferish, and had all the appearance of one who sleeps in the market at night and patronizes the catfish hotel by day. The confused state of his hair showed that he had an utter abhorrence of "slick" soap locks, and his beard looked as if it were rubbed off by a pummice stone instead of being operated on by a razor. His eyes were like two small golden fish in a basin of muddy water; his proboscis turned up like the toe of a Chinese shoe, and his mouth was like the opening of a Yankee's saddle bags.

"Cunniff," said the Recorder, "you were found lying drunk in Girod street last night, and very abusive."

"Vell," said Cunniff, "it aint no criminal offence to go on a kind of frolic, is it?"

"It is contrary to the city laws," said the Recorder, "and so long as you are a sojourner here we shall see that you do not violate them with impunity."

"Vell, but there aint nothin' in the constitution against goin' on a bender now and again, and therefore I say it's a wiolation of my wested rights to deprive me of personal liberty for committin' the hact."

"Mr. Cunniff," said the Recorder, "you have not been brought here to deliver an exposition of constitutional law, as you understand it—you are charged with being found drunk; for which offence I shall send you to the calaboose for thirty days."

Cunniff requested that he might be permitted to enter his solemn protest on the journals of the court, against a proceeding so subversive of the rights and liberties for which our fathers fought and bled.

"Take him out," said the Recorder.

The police officer instantly ushered him out; Cunniff, meantime, muttering something about "brief authority," "fantastic tricks," "high heaven," and "angels weeping."

September 17, 1840

Taking the Temperance Pledge

DAN INGLEMAN, a regular visitant of the watchman, was again up.

"What, here again, Daniel?" said the Recorder,

looking at Dan, after he had glanced at his name on the morning's report.

"Yes, Mr. Baldwin," said Dan, quite familiarly, "I'm hooked again, and it's very unfortunate—very, for I was just taking one jolification before I'd join the temperance society." [15]

"Why, you don't mean that, Dan?" said the Recorder.

"Fact as death," said Dan, "I was going right off to take the pledge when the watchman made a haul of me."

"But would you keep it?" said the Recorder.

"Would a Turk refuse to eat pork," said Dan—"to be sure I'd keep it."

"Well, then," said the Recorder, "we'll try the experiment"; and here he administered the teetotal pledge to Dan in open court, to be strictly observed and fulfilled for twelve calendar months.

"I want to introduce one proviso into that," said Dan, "before subscribing to it."

"What is it?" said the Recorder.

"Simply," said Dan, "that I may take the ardent if ordered it by a physician—or, in the absence of a physician, that I may take it when I feel I want it as a medicine."

---

[15] The temperance movement was strong and widespread at this time, and it had become a fad to take the pledge to abstain from strong drink.

The Recorder seemed to think that he would too often have recourse to it as a medicine, but, however, let him off on signing the pledge, subject to these conditions.

September 22, 1840

II

Them Charlies WILLIAM WALLIS, a stalworth,
stout customer, was among the prisoners yesterday morning. He lived below in the
Third Municipality, paid a visit yesterday to the Fau-
bourg St. Mary, and became so elated at the progress
of improvements which he witnessed that he went on
a regular bender. In bending his course towards home
on Monday night he of course fell on the banquette
and then fell into the clutches of a watchman. Although he was not able to walk, he was able to talk—
to sing. His song was to the air of "Scots wha ha," and

his voice sounded like a broken bassoon or a tin trombone. His song seemed to be got up expressly for the occasion, and no doubt at considerable expense. Here it is—

> Ye who would go on a spree,
> Ye who would get blue [1] with me,
> Ye who'd make a watchman flee,
> Come ye on with me.
>
> Now's the hour, and now's the night
> For a lock or for a fight,
> Now's the time for to get tight,
> Hurra for a jolly spree.

"That'll do," said Charley, "I s'pose you is an *ordinary* member of the anti-harmonican society—if you ain't you oughter be, for you is ordinary enough to be president of the ugly club."

"O, don't be kicking up such a d—d fuss," said Wallis, "or you'll be taken up by the Charlies. Them is the d—dest kind of fellows for nabbing chaps like you wot stays out late at night and get ginshingified. These here watchmen go to their death against drinking—I know *you* are high now—there, see how you stagger—take care of my nose—stand off, don't fall over me."

The watchman felt that language like his conveyed

---

[1] "To make blue is to die; but to get blue is not to die, it is only to get into a state of hallucination." *Picayune,* August 30, 1840.

not a personal offence to himself in particular, but that it was a libel on the good name of the fraternity in general. He therefore, without preface, prologue or comment, took Wallis to the watch house.

Wallis acknowledged the corn of being corned last night to the Recorder, and his honor discharged him on paying jail fees.

September 23, 1840

A Sailor Man on Land JACK ROBINSON, a tarpaulin-faced, tempest-tossed mariner, wearing large canvass trousers, a blue jacket with white pearl buttons in close column and double file, and a small sized glazed hat, was one of the prisoners before Recorder Baldwin yesterday. His hair was like a deck mop, his forehead like a companion ladder, his nose like a quadrant, his eyes like a pair of revolving lights seen in the distance, and his mouth was like the large end of a speaking trumpet. His left cheek was distended out in a conical shape, the effect of an enormous quid of tobacco that was stowed away inside.

The watchman boarded him in Gravier st.—His rudder was broken and he had lost his compass, or what was about the same thing, if he had one he was not able to use it. He was lurching about from one side of the street to the other, and singing—

"I'm now, d'ye see, six days on shore,
And yet my spree, it is not o'er;
Should I be calaboosed, wouldn't that be a bore?"

"I'll be d—d if it wouldn't," said Jack Robinson.

"Vell, you is in for it this time, *sure,* my covey,"
says Charley, laying his grappling irons on Jack Robinson—"you'll hammock in the calaboose, to-night,
old feller; that's as sure as that you have eat chowder."

"Avast there, you piratical looking old landshark," says Robinson, "or I'll douse your glims while
you'd be saying Jack Robinson." Jack, suiting the action to the word, made a blow at the guardian of the
night, missed him, and keeled over. The watchman,
without holding further parley with him, took him to
the Baronne street prison, *vi et armis.*

"Jack Robinson?" said the Recorder, in his usual
grave tone.

"Aye, aye, sir," said Robinson, standing up, giving
a jerk to his canvass trousers, removing the deposits
of tobacco from one jaw to the other, and giving himself a shake like a Newfoundland dog after leaving
the water.

"What do you follow for a living?" said the Recorder.

"Well, look here, commodore," said Jack Robinson, "if so be as you are quizzing me when you ask
that ere question, hard weather to me if I'll answer it.

I thinks as how it needs no telescope to tell I follows the sea; why, bless your eyes, I haint been off it a whole month since I first joined with Commodore McDonough.[2] The poor commodore has gone to Davy Jones' locker long since, and as brave a fellow he was as ever paced a quarter deck." Here the old tar's eye became moist, a tear stood in the corner of it, and he wiped it off with the cuff of his jacket.

"What ship do you belong to?" said the Recorder.

"Schooner Experiment," said John—"rather a rum 'un to look at, but a precious good sailer."

"Well, I shall let you go this morning," said the Recorder, "but when you next come on shore you ought to try some other experiment than that of getting drunk."

"Thank your honor," said Jack Robinson; "I'll make an entry of your advice in the logbook of my memory—it may keep me off from breakers in future." He clapped his low-crown hat on his head and put out.

September 24, 1840

Fancy Ladies   THERE were several prolix suits before the Recorder yesterday. Among others brought up there was a bevy of frail fair ones

---

[2] Thomas Macdonough (1783–1825) first won recognition in the Mediterranean, with Decatur and Bainbridge; but his chief fame rests on his victory over the British in 1814 in the battle of Lake Champlain.

from Marais street. Their names as called over by
the Recorder, were Georgianna Baltzell, Eliza Jane
Taylor, Eliza Devoy, Caroline Molton, and Eliza
O'Brien. They were all dressed richly and fashion-
ably; some wore quilled muslin bonnets, others cot-
tage straw bonnets; some were attired in mulberry
colored silk dresses, others in black silk; some of them
sported kid gloves, the finger casings of others were
of open network silk; some had on prunella boots,
others showed off morocco slippers; some wore their
hair in romantic corkscrew curls, others had their locks
drawn back *à la Chinoise;* all of them wore large dark
veils, and a superfluity of finger rings of the richest
kinds, inlaid with precious stones of the most rare
colors. The charge against them was being lewd and
abandoned women. Some persons may find fault with
the police for bringing such characters into the public
court, but we

> Think 'tis well to shut—at least, sometimes—
>   These women up—because in sad reality
> Their chastity in these Southern climes
>   Is not a thing of an astringent quality.

Their lawyer defended them with much tact and
professional skill—he spoke with as much pathos as
if he were reciting a monody to injured innocence.
To him the character of his clients served nothing—
his cause was everything; but it was a part of his system.

He was a man who had seen many changes,
  And always changed as true as any needle;
His polar star being one which rather ranges,
  And not the fixed; he knew the way to wheedle.

And so he did wheedle, and argue and allege, until with his own endeavors, the evidence of some "nice young men," and the dames' appearance, *prehaps*, he got three of them cleared, and the trial of two postponed to a future day.

Georgianna Baltzell, on leaving the office courtsied most gracefully to the court, but before doing so partly concealed her face in veil. Her bright eyes were scarcely to be seen—

Though if between the folds but one eye shone,
Like Sheba's Queen she vanquished with that one.

Eliza Jane Taylor was more pensive—more of a melancholy cast of countenance than her fair companion Miss Baltzell; dissipation had furrowed her once smooth brow, and dulled the lustre of her whilom bright brown eye. She had

That tone—those looks so changed—the withering
    blight
That sin and sorrow leave whe'er they light.

Caroline Molton differed in appearance from either of them, being neither as coquettish as the one nor as sentimentalish as the other.

Her form had all the softness of her sex,
    Her features all the sweetness of the d—l
When he put on the cherub to perplex
    Eve, and paved (God knows how) the road to evil.

Eliza Devoy's beauty lay in her finely chiselled, symmetrical and well proportioned form—

A form such as nature moulds when she would vie
With Fancy's pencil, and give birth to things
Lovely beyond its fairest picturings!

Eliza O'Brien, though last not *least*, was—was a "buster."

September 26, 1840

A Silent Partner

THE company assembled in the dock of Recorder Baldwin's court, yesterday, had among them a silent partner, who caused no little amusement to the open-mouthed auditory outside the bar, and to the more favored few who had seats inside. He was a Frenchman and a loafer, two characters rarely combined in the same person—we mean a loafer in the levee sense of the term, an anti-soap society man, not one of your mustached, elf-lock Count Humbug loafers, they are plenty as patriotism at a political meeting—but a cabaret-lounging, sleep-in-the-market loafer is hard to be caught, and such a one was our hero. His patronymic was Romai; he looked as dirty as a dredging machine, and as brown as a coffee mill.

"Antonia Romai," said the Recorder.

Romai seemed lost in a reverie of abstraction, and paid no attention to the calm and distinctly pronounced call of the court. One of the peace officers thinking that the prisoner was not treating the court with due respect, went up to him, gave him a shake as if he had been acted on by an electrifying machine, and placed him standing up. Romai being now on his legs the Recorder called "Watchman McDermott?"

A voice outside answered, "Here, sir," and the owner of that voice, one of the "finest pisantry in the world," shuffled up to the bench.

Recorder—McDermott, for what did you arrest this man?

McDermott—What man, yer anor? Is it that japanned face little blackguard there in the box that looks like a snuff seller's sign?

Recorder—He, standing up there!

McDermott—O, the thieving little *leprehaun*; it's meself that has law and raisen [reason] on me side for arristin' him.

Recorder—What was he saying?

McDermott—Sayin? purshumin to the word he was sayin at all at all, good, bad, or indifferent. Be gor he was as mute as a bagpipe that 'ud lose the wind, or as Thaddy Nowlan's cow when she got choked at the paytee pit.

Recorder—What was he doing?

McDermott—O, the divil a hapurth; he was as idle as a milestone, and looked as shy as a horse in a pound. O, he's a decayvin rascal.

Recorder—But if he was neither saying or doing anything, why did you arrest him?

McDermott—O, there it is, you see; that's the saycret of our purfession, that's the philosophy, as Brian Horan, the schoolmaster—the Lord be good and marciful to his sowl in glory—said, that's the philosophy of a watchman's business.

Recorder—I don't want to hear what Brian Horan said. I ask you why did you arrest him if he was not saying nor doing anything?

McDermott—Well, be gogstyinnagers, I believe yer anor thinks I am as green as an Irish shamrock. Why did I take him? why, af coorse I tuck him because he wasn't sayin or doin anything at all at all. How did I know but he was plottin trayson agin the state, or thinkin over in his own mind how he'd upset the constitution—how could I know it when he wouldn't tell me? the nastly little bullfrog of a munseer. I defy Councellor O'Connell himself to say I wasn't right in takin him up—parfecly right. Why did I take him? I took him up bacause he *could* give no account of himself.

Recorder—Stand aside, McDermott.

During this dialogue the prisoner stood in the dock as still as a statue.

Recorder—to the prisoner—What business do you follow?

No answer.

"Mr. Lafonta," said the Recorder to his Secretary, "speak to him in French."

Mr. Lafonta—*Que faites vous pour vivrer?* (What do you do for a living?)

No answer.

Recorder—Captain Harper, perhaps it is Spanish only he understands—ask him in Spanish what he follows for a living.

Capt. Harper—*Que hace vu para vivir?*

The prisoner was still mum.

"Try him at Dutch—he looks like a Dutchman," said some one. "He looks more like a Dutchman's pipe," said some one else. Mr. Ellis, the sergeant-at-arms to the Council was however sent for. He came, was instructed in his duty, and adjusting his glasses on his nose and looking through them at the prisoner, proceeded in his effort to draw an answer from him— *Wie ferdienen sie thr broth?*

The prisoner is silent.

Mr. Ellis—*Sprechen sie Deutsch?*

Not a word from the prisoner.

"By got, Mynheer Baldwin," said Mr. Ellis, "he pe no Dutchman—no whay."

Every one in the court in general now began to look with wonder on the prisoner, and to anticipate some

severe punishment for his outrageous contempt of
court, whilst the prisoner looked at no one in particular. What was to be done? "He's an Irishman,"
said one. "An Irishman!" said McDermott, the
watchman, "pursumin to the dhrap of Irish blood in
his vayns no more nor there is poteen whiskey in pure
Shannon water."

It was thought, notwithstanding the opinion so de-
cidedly expressed by McDermott that he *might* be an
Irishman, and officer O'Leary was commissioned to
feel his national pulse.

"Caud a ghenuin thú chan dá vahaha de ahll?" said
O'Leary, in a rich though somewhat smoothed down
Munster brogue, which being interpreted means,
"What do you do for a living?" Not an approach to
a reply on the part of the prisoner.

Now the game was blocked! No it wasn't though.
Commissary Barry just came into court, and as a last
effort to cause the prisoner to define his position, it
was decided that Mr. B. should address him in the
dead languages. "The *dead* languages!" said McDermott, who seemed to take a most lively interest in the
case—"O, be the hill of Howth—and that's a large
oath—if that bit of an apology for a man has any
language at all at all, it is as dead in him as a door
nail, and he seems to be as bothered as a quarins." [3]

[3] A kind of rustic corn mill.

"Silence," said the Recorder—"Mr. Barry, ask the prisoner in Latin what countryman he is."

The Commissary laid his brown beaver on the table, walked deliberately over to the dock, and in a tone as dignified as if it came from one of the professors of Harvard University, said—*"Unde venies? a quo regione venis?"* the English translation of which is—"What countryman are you? What do you do for a living?"

The prisoner still maintained his imperturbable silence, and all means seemed exhausted to draw a statement or confession from him.—Lieut. Winters here held a brief conference with the Recorder, after which his honor ordered him down for thirty days.

The secret for Romai's silence was now explained. He is both *deaf* and *dumb*, and consequently *could* give no account of himself, as McDermott, the watchman, so correctly stated in his report. He was known to the police, however as a "prigger," or Levee thief, and this accounts for the sentence passed on him by the Recorder.

September 30, 1840

Mistaking a Lamp-Post

THE windowed raggedness of Henry Widenbuck's clothes made him look like a target— firing at which, misfortune had wasted much powder.

On Wednesday night his ideas became somewhat confused, and his brain somewhat bewildered—he stretched out his hand to shake hands with a lamp-post.

"Do, my dear fellow," he said, "give me thy hand; let us embrace—we are men—we are brothers! You as well as I, must have drawn a blank in the lottery of Fortune, or you would not be the sport of the winds such a night as this. Again, I say—let us embrace!" and he flung his arms most affectionately round the lamp-post. Immediately he withdrew them, saying— "Sir, you're an unfeeling brute! an *un*sympathising scoundrel, sir! I address you like a gentleman, and you don't condescend to speak to me, sir! I offer you my hand, and you won't shake it, sir! I throw out my arms to embrace you, sir, and you allow me to grasp your cane! You are—you are—you are, —and you may go—you may go—you may go to"—

"To the watch-house," said Charley, coming up, "where you must go."

"Why didn't you speak to me at first?" said Widenbuck.

"Oh, shut up, and come along," said Charley— "you has got the man with the *fire iron*."

He took Widenbuck to the watch-house, and the Recorder gave him thirty days.

October 23, 1840

III

Scotland vs. Ireland

As THE election excitement increases, so does the sale of whiskey punches, and so do the prisoners at the police office. Why the effect follows the cause we are not metaphysicians enough to divine, and therefore content ourselves by stating the facts. On Saturday night two men were arrested by a cabbage-faced Dutch watchman: the one was a tall Scotchman, with legs as long as a surveyor's instrument, and a nose speckled like Scotch plaid: the other was a dumpy potato-faced Irishman—each of them had a "wee drap in his 'ee," and each was as full of love for fatherland, as an inflated balloon is full of gas.

"To the d—l I bob you and Scotland," said the Irishman, "sure it's no counthry at all at all—nor never was. Where was Scotland, I'd like to know, whin there was no one in Ireland but saints, and kings, and princes? and no houses, but all castles, that neither ould Nick nor ould Nol could make a braych in?"

"Weel, weel, Mr. O'Toole," said the Scotchman, "it is nae the cock, or the rooster, as folks here ca' him—it is na the rooster, I say, that craws loodest that maks the best fight. Auld Scotland was a'ways where she is noo mon—that is just ayont the Tweed."

"O, ye're an uncivilized set of haythens, any how," said Mr. O'Toole. "Hav'nt ye always ran wild through the Highlands, like Ingins, without as much as a bit of a breeches on yer legs?"

"I acknowledge we have, Mr. O'Toole, and so ha' the ancient Romans—they wore nae breeks when they conquerred the world," said the Scotchman, whose name, we should before have told our readers, was Sandy MacPherson.

"Thin, where's your national music? where's your harp?—the're both like Brien Flanagan's cow, when she got drown'd in the bog-hole—faith the're missin'."

"They're nae sick a thing," said MacPherson, "we ha goot oor Highland bagpipes, and it can stir up the bluid of a Scotchman any day as weel as your harp."

"O, Holy Moses!" exclaimed O'Toole, "d'ye call

the noise made by that *bresna* of sticks music! why, be jabers, I'd put a turkey-cock under my arm, catch his bill between my fingers, and make him play as good music as your bagpipes any day:—music! well, if that isn't takin' a liberty with the king's English, there's no shamrocks in Ireland. The Scotch fiddle is the only instrument, that I know of, ye can lay any claim to!"

"Vera weel, vera weel," said MacPherson, "let us nae quarrel aboot it."

"Well thin, why don't ye *whist?*" said O'Toole, " don't be makin' a Judy Fitzimmons of yerself. I suppose you'll be afther tellin' me that yer poetry is as good as ours too!"

"Yes, and I'll maintain it too," said MacPherson, evincing some warmth of manner for the first time.

"You can't," said O'Toole, "no more than you can stop the Shannon with a pitchfork."

MacPherson thought he could, and was determined he would; so from the composition of the

Lyric singers of that high soul'd land,

he made a selection from his favorite, Robby Burns, and commenced singing at the top of his voice,

"O Thou, my muse! guid auld Scotch drink,
   Whether thro' wimpling worms jink;
Or, richly brown, ream o'er the brink
       In glorious faem
Inspire me, till I lisp and wink,
       To sing thy name."

"Stop that," said O'Toole, "jist drop it like a hot prayta, if you wish to have your head whole; that's a national reflection—it conveys a double on-ton-dray, as the French say; it's an insinuation against Irish potheen, the shuperiority of which, above all other liquors, never was questioned before," and he began singing louder than the Scotchman, if not sweeter,

"There's not in the wide world, a liquor yet known,
 That's as good as the potheen as famed Innesshoun,"

when a Dutch watch-man came up, who looked like a mammoth locomotive head of cabbage, and said, "sthop that tam noise—what be for makin' such fush?"

"You be d—d, old leather head," said O'Toole; "be carefu', be carefu', Charley," said MacPherson, "that you dinna go ayont the bounds o' your duty: if I ken the constitution rightly, it says naething aboot the impropriety of folks crooning a song in the public streets."

"I whants no law from no one but the Recordher," said the Dutchman; he struck the curb stone, put the pair of worthies under arrest, and marched them to the watchhouse. MacPherson, when there, complained of the act as a wanton outrage on his personal liberty, and O'Toole said that his Milesian blood was ready to gush from his veins when he thought of it.

When they got out they forgot their mutual national antipathies, and conjointly heaped maledictions on the leather heads of all watch-men in general, and on that of the Dutch watch-man in particular.

November 3, 1840

Trying an Experiment JAMES BELTON figured yesterday among the prisoners. He was dressed in a full suit of domestic cloth, and had "honesty" written legibly on his forehead.

"Belton," said the Recorder, "you were found drunk on the Levee last night."

"I knock under, squire," said Belton.

"It was twelve o'clock," said the Recorder.

"And no mistake," said Belton.

"You had $826 in money about you," said the Recorder.

"That's the amount, to a cent," said Belton.

"Why did you get drunk, having so much money in your possession?" asked the Recorder.

"Because, squire," said Belton, "I'm just come from Illinois. I heard much about Orleans—much about its robberies and ropers-in. I have a heart myself—an honest heart. I didn't believe that New Orleans, or the people of New Orleans, are as bad as they are represented. I don't believe the world is as bad as it is sometimes painted. I believe that, like me, every man has a heart, an honest heart. I know this idea of mine is considered an erroneous, visionary one; but a Mohammedan does not more strictly believe in the Alcoran, than I do in the principle that all men are honest. I was anxious to test my principle; and with the view of doing so, I put that money in my pocket, and I put liquor in my mouth to steal away my brains. Now, squire, is not the proof so far on my side—is not my theory correct?—Some gentleman took my money from me, but are you not prepared to return it to me?"

The Recorder told him he was, deducting from it ten dollars of a fine for being intoxicated. He also told him he had not that high opinion of the honesty of mankind in general and particular which he (the prisoner) had: and cautioned him against trying the experiment again, lest, to his cost, he might find himself mistaken.

November 10, 1840

[Alas, he was soon in court again, a slicker "acquaintance from Illinois" having robbed him of some, and two more "benders" relieved him of all the rest but about $80.—Ed.]

When Low Was High

HENRY Low had been arrested the previous night for being high. He pushed along and kept moving up Magazine street, singing—

> I'm no politician, nor ever shall be—
> The joy of my life is to go on a spree
> Whoever is President is all one to me,
> While I can get gloriously corned.

"Don't be making such a noise," said Charley.

"I'll make as much noise as I d—d please," said Low— "What is the reason I should not? Don't high pressure steamboats make noise? don't locomotives make noise? don't stump speakers make noise? and don't my old woman make all kinds of a noise? Now, sir, is this a free country? am I a freeman? haven't I the same liberty of speech that my old woman has, though I have a vote and she haint got ne'er a one? Can a steamboat and a locomotive, and a cannon on a trainin' day, and a watchman's rattle at night, carry on just as they please, and must I be muzzled for singing a song? Is this law—is this equity—is this justice—is this liberty? Aint I of as much consequence as a steamboat or a locomotive, in the eyes of the law? But I knew it would be so. I knew when once Harrison got elected that our liberty would be swamped. Freemen to the rescue! Will you allow a blow to be struck at your liberties, through me?—Charge, friends, charge!"

Whether it was that the friends of Mr. Low, to whom he made so impassioned an appeal, were bound in the chains of Morpheus—or whether it was that they did not look on his arrest as a matter of as much importance as he did himself, we do not know; but certain it is that they were deaf to his call. None of them came to the rescue, and the only charge made was that by the watchman in handing over Mr. Low to the officer of the night.

Low promised amendment yesterday morning, and was discharged on paying jail fees.

November 18, 1840

Tennessee Impatience EDWARD COMMERFORD appeared to feel by no means at home in the prisoners' dock yesterday morning. The Recorder took his seat at a later hour than usual, and Ned, while he awaited his arrival, elbowed the prisoner to his right, poked his head back against the nose of the man in his rear, and made a sleepy looking loafer to his left cry out, "Oh! my corns!"

"Where's the Squire?" said Ned—"is he come? will he never come?"

"Silence," said the officer.

"I can't hear you," said Ned, "but I want to be heard in my own defence. The constitution guarantees a quick trial, and I'll have it or there's no alligators in the Mississippi."

(The Recorder enters and takes his seat on the bench.)

"This is a devil of a pretty fix these fellows have got me in," said Ned.

"Silence," said the officer again.

"I'll speak to the Squire," said Ned, "if I die for it."

"What's the matter?" asked the Recorder.

"He's annoying the whole court," replied an officer.

"If I'm not tried right off," said Ned, "I'll bring an action for false imprisonment—that I will."

"Mr. Commerford, you were found lying drunk," said the Recorder, "and the watchman took you up and brought you to the watch house."

"O, that was remarkably kind of the watchman," said Ned, "but if I'm to be kept in confinement this way during the term of my natural life, I had much rather he had left me where I was."

"Pay your jail fees," said the Recorder, "and you may go."

"Squire," said Ned, "Squire, you're a horse and if ever I meet you up in Tennessee, in our diggins, I'll go the big figure in standing treat for all hands."

He paid fees and put out.

December 13, 1840

Patriotism   MILES WEST was the observed of all observers in the police office yesterday morning. He looked as dirty as though he had been used as a mud machine for deepening the mouths of the Mississippi, and as cold as a Lapland winter. He had an old United States flag wrapped around him, toga fashion, which made him present rather a ludicrous appearance.

"West," said the Recorder, "the watchman arrested you on the Levee last night. You were lying down and had a flag of the United States around you."

"I know it, I know it," said West, who suddenly seemed to be imbued with the spirit of eloquence— "I know it, sir, and I know that by that arrest the most sacred rights of a freeman were violated."

"Where did you get that flag," asked the Recorder.

"Get it?" said West, echoing the Recorder's interrogatory— "Why, sir, it was mine by right, by inheritance. I was born under it, have lived under it, and will die under it." (He sings):

"Oh! say can you see by the dawn's early light,
What we so proudly hailed at the twilight's last
  gleaming,
Whose broad stripes and bright stars—"

"Silence," said the police officer, "silence there!"

"More persecution," said West, "more persecution; but how can I expect to be free from it here, when it reached me as I lay last night wrapped in the folds of my country's flag."

"You were quite insensible at the time you were taken up," said the Recorder.

"Yes, I was insensible to fear," said West, making a grand flourish with his hand, as if he were exorcising some unseen spirit—"for I thought my country's ensign would have shielded me from offence or intrusion. I knew that its appearance has made sceptered despots tremble on their thrones and tyrants relinquish their schemes of oppression, and could I have supposed that it would not prove a barrier against the intrusive advances of a watchman? Why, may it please the court, in any land, or among any people, whether savage or civilized, I should look upon it as an aegis—a panoply that would render my personal liberty secure. Then why—why, in this my own, my native land, is its all-protecting influence set at defiance by a vulgar watchman?"

"The watchman did no more than his duty," said the Recorder.

"With deference to the court I say," replied West, "that he overstepped his duty, otherwise he would not have dared to lay his hands on me while enshrouded in the sacred emblem of my country's freedom. Why, sir, even in England, with its monarchy and its aristocracy and its heirarchy, an Englishman boasts that his house is his castle, and that the king dare not enter it. Does the flag under which our forefathers fought and conquered, I would ask, afford less protection to an American citizen than the cabin of an English peasant does to a British subject? That is the question, sir, that is the question," he said confidently, as if he had defined his position in a manner which admitted of neither doubt nor dissent.

"The question is," said the Recorder, unmoved by either the eloquence or the patriotic aspirations of West, "that you have been found drunk in the street in violation of our municipal laws—that the guilt of an action is neither extenuated nor palliated by the dress or insignia which the perpetrator may wear, and that you be fined five dollars—that's the question."

West folded his flag still more closely around him, paid the fine and went out.

December 22, 1840

Disadvantages of Laboring

"NEW ORLEANS is a good place, and it aint a good place," said Frank Smith, as he wended his way up by Lafayette Square on Monday night. From the manner in which this nullifying opinion of Frank's was delivered it was very evident that, situated as he was, he was most incompetent to deliver it, for he only maintained his equilibrium by holding on to the railing of the Square like a convict to a tread mill. "Yes," he continued, "it is and it aint. It's a first rate place in the vay of liquoring and lunches. I likes the atmosphere too. In the vinter season, if a feller can't find his change to pay for a bed, the inconvenience of sleepin' out is by no means as great as it is more north'ard. But then these here pryin' vatchmen—I'm blowed if I don't believe they have a sprinklin' of Spanish bloodhound in them, they do smell a feller out so; this here's the item vhat's to go to the debit side of living in New Orleans. Vatchmen has been my evil genius; I could get along in a genteel vay only for them—I say genteel, for if they'd let me apply my talent to loafin' I never need do no vork. Any feller as vorks can have no claim to respectability; it's like givin' up your effects to your creditors—you forfeit all claim to it, and vot's vorse it don't go for nobody's benefit. And see the consekvence of being picked up by these here Charlies; you are brought up before the Recorder, and because you doesn't follow some wulgar business he sends you to the calaboose for thirty days, and that is vot I calls cramping a feller's mind, clipping the vings of his genius, clapping manacles on his invention so far as all practical purposes are concerned. Ven he is vonce in it's all up vith him; he can't make no new acquaintances vot vould stand treat; he can't take his lunch and eleven o'clocker, and for the sake of convenience forget to pay for it. In a vord, he cannot illustrate his ideas of the credit system by reference to its advantages as personally known to himself."

Thus moralized, or soliloquized or philosophized Frank Smith, as he hung on to the railing of Lafayette

Square like a door on broken hinges in a windy day, when his evil genius—

"Why is you out so late?" asked Charley, gruffly.

"O, you is there, is you?" said Frank—"guessed I couldn't avoid being seen by you. I believes your eyes are made of the real, patent, portable gas that makes everything visible."

"O, it's you, is it?" said Charley, who now began to recognize his customer—"come along to the vatch 'us."

"Let me pass this time," said Frank.

"Not a bit of it," replied the watchman—"a *habee corpy* couldn't release you from me now," and in pursuance of his irrevocable determination he lodged Smith in the watch house.

The Recorder, as Frank anticipated, sent him down for thirty days.

December 23, 1840

IV

*A Night in
the Calaboose*

THERE were but a few "out-laters" up before the Recorder yesterday morning—Mick Bailey made one among them. Mick had just come down from St. Louis on a voyage of "diskivery," and from the manner in which he seemed to feel, if he should shortly get away he will not be in a very particular hurry to return here.

"Where do you live?" asked the Recorder.

"In St. Louis," replied Mick, "when I'm at home,

and I wouldn't care if I *war* at home now."

"What have you been doing?" asked the Judge.

"Nothin' at all at all," said Mick, "till I was taken into that black hole of a calaboose by some fellow that looked like a rusty buoy in a river."

"Well, what did you do when you got there?" asked the Recorder.

"Do," said Mick, "what could I do? I wasn't there as long as you'd be blowing the froth off a pint of beer, when I was robbed and murthered and kilt entirely. One fellow put his hand in me pocket— 'Murther!' sis I— 'Knock him down,' sis another, and it was no sooner sed than dun, for he give me as purty a tip of his twig over the hatband as iver I got in me life. 'Fair play is a jewel,' sis I; 'one at a time and I'm able to take the could out of any of yees'; but I might as well have been whistling jigs to a milestone—d—l a the layst attintion they paid to me, but pegged away at me till they robbed and murthered me, as I sed afore, and left me head as soft as that jintleman's that was layin' down law here awhile ago."

"Do you know the man that murdered you?" asked the Recorder.

"Man!" said Michael—"man! I beg yer anor wont add insult to injury by axin' me sich a question. D'ye think there's *one* man in Arlains that 'ud be able to lay me in this condition? (pointing to sundry wounds and contusions which adorned his physiognomy.) I give ye me word I was attacked simultaynously, one after another, by a whole regiment o' them, as ugly and as murtherin' lookin' as if they followed the killin' business for a purfession."

"Do you know any one in the city?" asked the Recorder.

"Why, thin, as a civil question requires a civil answer, I may as well tell you, plump and plain, that I don't know the sarra a one. I did know Brien Higgins, but he died of the yallow fayver, God rest his sowl! and betune you and me, when I looked at meself today in the glass I didn't know meself, I was so Matty-Murphy'sd, as the schoolmaster used to call a sudden change of faytures."

The Recorder told Mick that he should remand him until some person would be found to know him, or at least until he would know himself.

December 31, 1840

Two Benighted Lovers CHARLEY GALLAGHER and Catharine Gallagher *alias* Catharine Lacey, "two young lovers," went on a pleasure ramble on Sunday evening, and the moments flew so swiftly and pleasantly that they were benighted erè they knew it.—Their thoughts were not on time, and we expect not on eternity, either. They were thinking of *love;* looking up among the bright stars, and dreaming of the Elysian fields, and Adam; (and Eve too—for what was Adam without Eve? and what is Charley Gallagher without Catharine Gallagher *alias* Catharine Lacey?) they were thinking of Cupids and Venuses, and wondering if they drank "mountain dew," and whether *praties* didn't grow in the garden of Paradise, and "all that sort o' thing," until, as we said before, night came upon them unawares, like a cat in the dark.

Catharine, by nature being very timid, was unwilling to venture back home at such a late hour, and being withal a little *fatagued,* she proposed to Charley to stop for the night on a neighboring gallery. The proposition was agreed to, and the "young lovers" were soon encircled in the arms of one Mr. Morpheus —for this old fellow reigns on the floor of a balcony as well as on feather beds and hair mattresses. But "the course of true love never did run smooth," and the blissful slumbers of Mr. Gallagher and Mrs. Gallagher *alias* Miss Lacey were suddenly disturbed by the impertinent intrusion of a prowling watchman. The loving couple were removed from their new-made lodgings to more secure quarters in the watch house, and the Recorder, after hearing their story, let them go.

July 28, 1840

What Harm Is There in a Bowie-Knife? THE regular business of the morning had been gone through with, when one of the officers discovered a chap, named Joseph Glendenning, in the crowd outside the bar with a large, glittering Bowie-knife projecting from under his vest. The officer very properly arrested the fellow and informed the Recorder. He was ordered to be brought in, and the knife was produced. It had on the blade, in glaring letters—"*Judge Lynch's Law!*" Recorder Baldwin did not think fit to allow Judge Lynch to preside in his court, and asked Glendenning what he brought such an instrument there for.

"I didn't bring it here for nothing," said Glendenning. "I want it for varmints; there's a great many varmints up my way and all about our parts."

"Where do you live?" asked the Recorder.

"On Sunflower river." [1]

"Well, you can't use such things in a civilized community. If you believe in Judge Lynch's law you must go back to Sunflower river."

"Oh, I don't know nothing about Judge Lynch, nor his law nuther. There's a heap of *bars* and sich like varmints up in our parts, and I wants sich a knife as that for them."

"You are liable to a fine for carrying this knife, of

[1] A stream in Mississippi flowing into the Yazoo.

not more than $100, nor less than $25. I'll make it the lowest, however, and if you pay it you can go."

The fellow, who appeared to be "more fool than knave," became alarmed at this, and actually cried. He said he was unable to pay the fine; had no money and was far from home; was willing to give up his knife; promised not to violate the law again; and begged the Recorder to release him.

After a reprimand the judge let him go.

July 30, 1840

Tea or No Tea, That Is the Question   Mr. Philip Powers and Mrs. Philip Powers were arrested for going through an amateur performance of the farce of "Family Jars," or, as the watchman vulgarly put it, for fighting and disturbing the peace.

It appeared that when Philip went in to take his *tay* in the morning, "the divil a dhrop of aither tay-tay or coffee-tay" was ready for him; the "kittle" was as "cowld" as a lump of Massachusetts ice; his "betther half" was fast asleep, and appeared to be giving imitations of Cioffi on the trombone with her nasal organ.

"Is the brickfist ready?" said Phil.

"Hould your whist, and don't disturb me dhrame," said his spouse.

"O dhrop yer goster," says Phil, " 'tis a burnin' shame for ye to be in bid at this hour of the blissed mornin', so it is, and the whole world up and at their work. Faix, it's a pity but ye wor an estated lady and had sarvints to wait on ye, and had nothin' to do at all at all, like a fine jontlewoman!"

"O ye brute baste!" said Mrs. P. "This is jist what I might expict whin I had any thing to do wid the likes o' ye!"

Thus they continued on, Mrs. P. returning a Roland for Philip's Oliver, till the uproar at length attracted the watchman and they were taken to the watch-house. It happened, singularly enough, that notwithstanding all this crimination and recrimination, neither of them had a complaint to make of the other at the watch-house, [and] they were therefore both discharged.

July 31, 1840

*Staying Awake
at an Irish
Wake*

PETER COFFIELD was found drunk. "Peter," said the Recorder, "you was drunk last night."

Peter—"Maybe I was and maybe I wasn't; if I was itself, how could I help it—I was at a wake, and whiniver I go to a wake it cums nat'ral to me."

"You don't drink at a wake, surely?" says the Recorder.

"Becourse I do," says Peter; "how would yer honor ixpict me to stay up all night widout takin' a little o' somethin' to dhrown grief? Not take anything at a wake? Well that 'ud be a purty way, indeed, to show respect for a dacent corpse. Faith, it's come to a purty time of day wid us if we are to be put in the calaboose for takin' a dhrop at a wake. I suppose it will soon come to that pass that there'll be no wake at all; and if ther niver was a wake there niver would be that beautiful political song about

Mrs. Blany, Mrs. Delany, Mrs. Fagan and McFoe, All driving off in style to the wake of Teddy Roe.

"It is not necessary that you should sing any more," says the Recorder; "pay your jail fees and you may go."

Peter was *thar* with his $1.37½, and cleared.

August 2, 1840

Clothes Make the Gentleman

CHARLES WELLS counted one among the prisoners who appeared before Recorder Baldwin on Sunday morning. He had been very *well* I thank you the night previous. Charley is a loafer, with a small sprinkling of the philosopher in his composition. Here are his "musings by the way" on Saturday night. "The veather is orful varm," said Charley, "that are a fact but the thermometer haint no effect on men's minds; it's an unfeelin, frosty vorld. People haint no feelin nor sympathy for a feller what haint got the awailable funds himself. He can't run his face for drinks no vhere, nor he can't 'come it' on the boarding house keepers, because he aint got no luggage. I'm just in that vay now, and I tell you vot it is, stranger, I'm in a bad fix—a desput condition. If I vas a gentleman I'd go and put up at some of the vaterin places for the summer. I'd start for Brandyvine Springs. I is a gentleman in all but the outvard appearance, and that is the most materialist point of all. Nature has done her own part—I haint no fault to find vith her, she has been wery liberal indeed—but the rascally tailor, vhat is as destitute of generosity as his goose is of feathers, has cut through her designs; he has cabbaged her ideas and spoiled the job, so here I is in an unfinished state, like the Bunker Hill monument, or the Jackson monument, or Plough's vashing machine, or any other great vork that haint been carried through; and all for a flash shoot of clothes, vithout vhich no man can be a gentleman, vhatever be his hintelects."

"Vhy," said the watchman, who had just come up, "von vould suppose as how you vas addressin an inwisible political meetin, you has got so much to say."

"Go on," said Charley Wells, to Charley the watchman, in a tone of assumed dignity—"go on, thou arrester of erring mortals."

"Vhy, you is blue," said the watchman—"you

ought to be ashamed of yourself to be in such a condition."

"Ashamed of my condition," said Wells, "Vhy," he
added—

'Honor and shame from no condition rise,
    Act well your part, there all the honor lies.'

"Well then, my covey," said the watchman, "I'll
take your adwice, and I'll take yourself to the vatchus
[watchhouse]—and that will be actin my part vell, if
I knows vot the important duty that dewolves on a
vatchman is—come on, old feller," and making a
prisoner of Charley Wells, he deposited his body in
Baronne street watchhouse.

The prisoner made a most philosophical appeal to
the Recorder, who let him off on paying jail fees.

August 11, 1840

Shaving a Shaver   A LITTLE FRENCHMAN, whose
hair stood on end *à la Jackson*,
with short legs and large calves, kicked up almost as
great a fuss in Recorder Baldwin's court yesterday,
as Louis Napoleon did recently in Boulogne. His nose
was as sharp as a razor, and his face was as white from
powder as if it were newly lathered. A large frill stuck
perpendicularly out from his bosom like an open ob-
long fan, and a large circular snuff box resembling the

Grand Humbug Real Estate Lottery Wheel, protruded from his vest pocket.

"You shave me, I shave you, eh? *sacre!* one great imposture," said the Frenchman, pulling his snuff box hurriedly from his vest pocket, giving it a wicked crack of his open hand on the lid, and raising a large pinch of the pungent powder to his nose between his two fingers and thumb, he snuffed up the lesser portion of it, the greater he let fall on his frill. "You shave me, I shave you, eh?" again he repeated, with as much apparent assurance of success in the suit he was about to engage in, as a politician speaks of the election of his favorite presidential candidate— "By gar, sacre, I shall let you see by de law wethare you shave me for I shave you, eh?" This was addressed to a man who, if he was not a worn out blackleg, looked extremely like one—and notwithstanding the little Frenchman's tempestuous passion, retained the most placid equanimity of temper.

"Have you any charge to make, sir?" said the Recorder to the little Frenchman.

"By gar, Monsieur Judge," said the little Frenchman, "I have only twelve months charge to make against dis dere robbere."

"If you bring it before this court," said the Recorder, "you will have to make it brief. I cannot occupy myself in hearing a twelve months' charge from you."

"Pardonnez moi, Monsieur Judge, you no comprehend. I am de one grand barbere, *freezuer* and *perruquier* from Par*ee;* dis man comes to my emporium of fashion and he says, what you pay me—no, sacre pay—what you charge me, he says, for barbering— for shave me, you call it, and cut my hair for one year? I do it, I said, and give you whiskers de grand Par*ee* curl for tirty dollar, but you pay me cash down—not no credit system for me, nevare."

"Well, did he comply with your terms?" said the Recorder.

"Not one time, he no paid me at all," said the Frenchman—"I now shave him one month and give his hair de fashionable cut and de finish off wid de bear's grease, and he never paid me one cent. Sacre! he be one grand wat you call—humbug—one shaver what don't be barbers you know, but wat live by shaving barbers and oder gentlemens. Sacre! when I ask him for my tirty dollar dis vera mornin', he give me tree ten dollar bills of de fallen in Brandon Bank,[2] and he say they be good as silver next year. *Mon Dieu! Mon Dieu!* they will nevare be no good till de whole world break up in one smash! What you say to dat, Monsieur Judge?" continued the little Frenchman, anxious to draw from the Recorder his opinion of the man who could have the effrontery to offer a Parisian barber $30 in Brandon money for cutting his

[2] One of the Mississippi banks which failed about this time.

hair and shaving him for twelve months, and giving his whiskers the grand curl—"wat you say to dat, Monsieur Judge, eh?"

"Why, I say it was anything but a legal tender," said the Judge, "and the very worst representative of a specie currency which he could offer you."

"I shave him, he want shave me," said the Frenchman, taking another large pinch of snuff.

The defendant was now called on to state what he had to say to the charge made against him. He admitted a part and denied a part. It was true, he said, that the Frenchman had shaved him for a month, powdered his face, cut his hair, rubbed in the bear's grease, till he thought the hair of his head would be mistaken for a grenadier's cap, it grew so strong, and he took excessive pains to curl his whiskers; but he emphatically denied offering to remunerate him with Brandon money. He merely pulled it out, he said, to show what a loss he sustained as a holder of it; and in proof that he did not do it as a fraud, he now offered to pay the barber in good and current Second Municipality bills for his services.

The proposition was accepted—the Frenchman's demand was liquidated, and he left the office snuffing his snuff, and saying in triumph to the defendant—"By gar, I can shave you, but you can no shave me, not no how—ha! ha!"

October 15, 1840

*What Do
You Follow?*

JOHN MURPHY was called up. John was taken up Sunday night in a state of intoxication. On Monday morning he was brought out, but was too drunk to stand a fair trial; he couldn't answer any questions, and was remanded. Yesterday he had cooled off and was as good as new. When John was called he got up and said— "Well, Mr. Baldwin, I'm ready for you now; what were you trying to talk about yesterday morning?"

"You were so drunk yesterday that you couldn't stand up. Are you sober to-day?" said the Recorder.

"I'm sober," said Murphy, "and ready to answer the questions of a Philadelphia lawyer."

"Well, what do you follow?"

"What do I follow? I follow a good many things. Sometimes, when I'm dry, I follow my inclination and take a drink; and sometimes—"

"Stop, sir—I want to know what you follow for a living?"

"Well, why didn't you say so? I follow making the 'staff of life'—in other words, I'm a baker—a *floury* sort of fellow."

The Recorder, being satisfied that John was a laboring man, let him go.

July 29, 1840

V

An Artist Paints a Picture As RECORDER BALDWIN was yesterday disposing of some case of ordinary importance, a low, chubby, cabbage-headed Dutchman and a thin, tall, attenuated man in a seedy black coat, pants to match, and a well-brushed faded silk hat enteɪed the office. The first notice of their presence which the court had was the Dutchman telling the tall, thin, attenuated gentleman in the seedy dress and faded silk hat, that he "wash a tam shon of a pitch."

At this wanton interruption of the general order of

67

the court, the Recorder cried "Silence!" and every officer in court echoed the order.

"What is the matter?" asked the Recorder.

"Vhy, here pe von tam imposthure vhat say he painted my shon, and it aint my shon, not at all, Got tam." Here the Dutchman looked sourkrout at the tall, thin gentleman in the seedy black suit with the faded silk hat.

The Dutchman got a hint to "shut up," from one of the officers, and was told if he did not treat the court with more deference, he would have to rusticate in the calaboose for twenty-four hours.

"Will you," said the Recorder, addressing the tall, thin man—"will you explain the matter at issue between this man, who seems inclined to be so noisy, and yourself. What is it that has brought both of you here?"

"I shall endeavor," said the tall, thin man in the seedy suit of black, "to comply with the request of the court; and although in the absence of any legal adviser I feel the weight of the responsibility which rests on me, yet trusting to the truth of my cause, to the enlightened and liberal feeling that pervades this court and this great community in every thing which relates to the fine arts, and firmly believing in this intellectual age when genius is fostered, when true taste is appreciated, when brilliant talents are succored and encouraged—in a word, may it please the court, when mind predominates over mere matter—I fearlessly enter on the task which the court has imposed on me, fearless of the results when I have no one to combat but the vegetable individual—the animated pumpkin who now stands by my side."

"Got tam," said the Dutchman.

"Silence!" said the officer. And the man in the seedy suit proceeded.

"As I was saying to the court," continued the man who looked like a target—"my picture of the transaction, like all which I have ever drawn, shall be lifelike. I shall use only the brush of truth, and my coloring shall be natural and in strict accordance with facts. —The part which I have acted in the affair, will, I am sanguine to say, furnish one with *light*. This individual's conduct,"—pointing to the Dutchman— "supplies more than a sufficient share of shade."

"Have you any complaint to make?" asked the Recorder, appearing somewhat tired of listening to the speech of the tall, thin man which smelt strongly of vermilion, black lead and yellow ochre.

"Ah," said the tall, thin man, "there's the rub. Allow me for one moment to *brush* up my memory, and I shall an 'unvarnished tale deliver' of the transaction."

"You tam humpug," said the Dutchman in a tone which did not reach the bench.

"My name, may it please the court," said the tall,

thin man, "is Jones—Sylvester Jones, at the service of the court. I am a professor of the fine arts, or as it is vulgarly called, a painter. I am a F. R. S., and R. A., and an A. S. S. This individual here, whose name, as well as I can pronounce it, is Johan Vonhickenslaughter. What an abominable, unpoetical name!"

"No matter about the euphony of the name," said the Recorder. "What has he done?"

"Why," said the artist, "he employed me to make a portrait of his eldest son, a mere human animalculum I assure you, with no more expression in his face than there is in a peeled turnip. Well, of course I gave a life-likeness of the boy. My great forte is in catching the expression of the eye and the muscles of the mouth, but d—n me— (beg the court's pardon)—he, I say, had no expression to catch.—Well, I took the picture home, and would the court believe it, instead of paying me for it, this individual offered me personal violence because his son's portrait did not resemble a picture of the younger Bonaparte, which he had hanging up in his room, and whom, he says, his son resembles, ha! ha! ha!—Beg the court's pardon again, but really— cannot avoid laughing at the individual's idea—a perfect monomania, I assure you."

"Got tam, doesh you shay dat pe like my shon? It ish like not no one, Got tam." Here the Dutchman exhibited what the artist called a perfect likeness of Mrs. Vonhickenslaughter's first born, but which was in truth

as like an antiquated Dutch doll, Admiral Vonbroom,
or a pair of twin apples grafted together, as it was like
the human face divine of either the young Dutchman
or any one else.

"Whesh mhy shon's nose, or mhy shon's eyhs, or
mhy shon's red cheeks? Got tam," said the Dutchman
as he pointed to where those different features should
be on the painting.

The Recorder said he was not prepared to say what
were the talents of the artist, or how far his own account of his professional abilities was correct, but he
certainly did not look on the picture exhibited as a *chef
d'œuvre* in the way of portrait painting, nor could he
undertake to tell how nearly it resembled the original,
as the amiable youth whose likeness it purported to be
was not present. As there was no actual assault proven
he refused to grant a warrant, and dismissed the parties, advising Mr. Vonhickenslaughter to permit little
Vonhickenslaughter to set once more to Sylvester
Jones, the artist.

The Dutchman left the office, swearing that no
"tam humpug should nhever phaint hish shon."
"Mhy shon," he said, "ish like young Bhonaparte,
put that phicter whashn't like nhopody, Got tam."

October 10, 1840

Political Disputation FRANK SMITH and Thomas
Reddin were up before Re-
corder Baldwin on Sunday morning. They were ar-
ested for being noisy and intoxicated.

"Smith," said the Recorder, "about what did you
and Reddin quarrel?"

"Vy, about the old thing, your honor," said Smith.

"What do you call the old thing?" said the Recorder.

"Vy, this here presidential helection," [1] said Smith.

"O, you differ in politics, do you?" said the Recorder.

"Certainly ve do," said Smith—"he is a *rabbit* loco
foco [2] and I is a vig [whig]."

"A what?" said the Recorder.

"A wiolent politician and in favor of Wan Buren,"
said Smith. "But I'll tell your honor as how it is. Ve
both lives in the same yard, and venever I passes him
he says there goes Hard Cider; [3] there is von of the
party wot aint got no principles; there's a supporter of
the man wot's been made brave by certificates and not

[1] This was the campaign of 1840, in which William Henry Harrison, the Whig, was opposing Martin Van Buren, the Democrat.

[2] A name applied to the radical wing of the Democratic Party in
New York in 1835, and later used derisively for the whole party.

[3] Someone derisively said of Harrison, the Whig candidate in
1840, that if he were given a barrel of hard cider he would sit the
remainder of his days in a log cabin. Thereupon the Whigs seized
upon a log cabin and hard cider as symbols to capture the popular
imagination.

by his sword; [4] and he goes on in that ere vay vich no good vig can stand. Ven he finds the other vigs out what live in the yard and the loco focos at home, he is sure to take the wote and then he calls it a Wan Buren wictory and a sign of the times, and all that. The fact is, your honor, if the feller vasn't looking out for an office I doesn't think he'd be half as patriotic as he is."

"Reddin," said the Recorder, "is your conduct such as Smith describes it?"

"Not a bit on it," said Reddin—"if I vas to be let alone I'd never do nothing to nobody, but he's heternally talking politics. Ven my old voman locks the door and goes out, he makes a fox on it vith chalk and writes underneath it, 'this here is Sly Reynard, from Kinderhook, vot vos for sometime in the London Zoological Gardens, but now is in the Menagerie at Vashington; he's the most cunning hanimal vot's known to naturalists.' [5] This is not all, your honor. Ven I vants to sleep at night I'm blowed if I can get a vink, he kicks up such a rumpus, singing Harrison songs the whole time and crowing like a reg'lar rooster.[6] I have challenged him over and over again, but I never can get him to toe the mark, no how."

"Do you know," said the Recorder, "that by chal-

---

[4] Harrison's military career was not as impressive as the Whigs tried to make it appear.

[5] Van Buren's astute political activities caused him to be likened to a fox.

[6] The rooster was the Democratic symbol.

lenging him you have been guilty of inciting to a breach of the peace."

"I doesn't mean a duel, your honor," said Reddin, "but to a discussion of principles; but I'm blamed if I don't believe he haint got any."

"But can't you both retain your respective political opinions without quarreling?" said the Recorder.

"Vell, then," said Reddin, "your honor must bind him over not to sing Arrison songs between the hours of ten o'clock at night and six o'clock in the morning, and not to be frightening my children out of bed by firing off that old rusty musket in celebration of wictories when he haint gained none. Yes, and prewent him, your honor," continued Reddin, "from making his big dog stand on his hind legs in my presence, and saying, as he points to him, 'here is von of Wan Buren's present standing harmy'; nor I wont stand no more from him about negro testimony, cause it's all gammon."

On the part of Smith it was provided that Reddin was not to call him a hard cider cask nor a worshipper of log cabins, any more. They made mutual promises to act with more forbearance toward one another in future, and to display a greater degree of political charity than they have evinced heretofore, and were discharged.

October 13, 1840

Mistaking a Charley

THE oddest looking fellow up before the Recorder yesterday was Jack Burns. He was a case of the superlative order, or highly concentrated kind. His eyes were like a pair of preserved beans; nature had made an excavation in the centre of his nose; his lips were like a large plum that became cracked at the center from being over ripe; there was a hollow in his chin as if it had been made there by a butter taster; his hair was like a half-tanned fox skin, and his whole face was as ragged as a newly picked mill-stone.

He was progressing along the Levee, if the term can be applied to making three steps forward, two to the right, four to the left, and an uncertain number backward. The motion of his tongue, like the motion of his feet, went every which way. He was singing, and whilst one of his notes was at D flat the next one jumped clear up to A sharp. The watchman could not positively swear to what tune his song went, but from the measure we would say that it was to the air of "Roy's wife of Aldavallah."—Thus it went:—

> Though I go upon the batter,
> To others it should make no matter;
>   Yet if I get high,
>   Some watchman spy
> Says, shut up—why make so d—d a clatter?

"And then," said Burns, descending from poetry to prose, "he is sure to lay his grappling irons on me and take me right off to the watchhouse."

"He does, does he," said the watchman, who had been listening to the melody of Burns.

"I'm blamed if he don't," said Burns, "and I'll tell you what it is, old feller, I look upon these here Charlies, both indiwidually and in the aggregate, as greater enemies to human happiness and the peace of society, than either mosquitoes or the Seminole Indians. I'm blow'd if I doesn't have a law of general hextermination passed agin all vatchmen and vatchmen's rattles by the next Congress. They are the nat'ral enemies of the 'uman race, and I wants to put a general hextinguisher on 'em."

"The d—l you do," says Charley, who became somewhat enraged at this wholesale denunciation of his whole "order." "Well now, I tell you one thing, old feller, you can't shine, no how you can fix it. Now, if you aint no objection you'll come along with me, and we'll see to-morrow how far you can carry out your principles."

"Why, you haint no vatchman," said Burns.

"Yes, but I are though," said Charley, "and a right up and down one at that."

"Vell," said Burns, "you know I didn't mean vhat I said—I vas but larkin'."

"I aint green," said Charley. "You can't throw sand

in this child's eyes. I can't stand no more nonsense: business is business, as the Yankee said when he dived into the pumpkin pie; so come along." And off he took Burns to the Baronne street watchhouse.

As they went along the prisoner took much pains to convince his captor that the watchmen, taken as a body, or every body among them taken as himself, were the best-disposed fellows in the world—the protectors of men's lives and liberties, and in fact whole-souled fellows in every sense of the word.

Charley was not to be caught in the trap, so he delivered Burns in "good order and condition" to the constable of the night at the Baronne street prison, where he was caged till yesterday morning.

Before the Recorder he pleaded good intentions, but his honor having recognized him as one who had been up before and down before, to prevent him from being up again he sent him down again for thirty days.

October 9, 1840

The Parts of Speech

ALEXANDER PERSSE, a man who looked like a long used, badly bound edition of Essays on Intemperance, was found "on the shelf," or rather on the banquette in Phillipa street, on Wednesday night. He was "very well, I thank you." Persse teaches the young idea how to shoot; but finding that he could not keep pace, we suppose, with the march of intellect, he lay himself down on the banquette, either to store his mind with new inspiration or to arrange the ideas with which his mind was already stored, and prepare for another start off in the intellectual race.

"Who is here?" said the watchman when he came up to Persse, stirring him up with his long pole—"Who's here?"

"I am, thou art, he, she or it is," said Persse, launching at once into the sea of his vocation, and taking the tone of his language from the "shop."

"You is high," said the watchman.

"I deny, sir, that I am high," said Persse— "All our authors, sir, who have written on the language, agree in saying that high is an adjective, because, sir, it expresses a condition or quality; now, sir, I am Alexander Persse, a noun—a noun proper, sir, of the first person, masculine gender, singular number—see here, old fellow, let us drink—and I am—I am, sir, nominative case to the verb drink. Now, sir, confess your error when you say I am high—am a mere adjective."

"Come along to the watch house," said Charley.

"No, sir," said Persse, "I shall decline it, and in a manner strictly in accordance with the principles of etymology; thus, sir, come, came, come. Now, sir, the conjugation is equally simple, thus—I come, thou comest, he, she, or it cometh or comes."

"This here's all nonsense," said Charley, who was getting out of patience with the learned grammarian.

"Yes, sir," said Persse, "you are perfectly right; nonsense is a kind of compound word, combining both a negative and an affirmative—this, sir, is one of the idioms peculiar to our language."

"I wont hear no more of it," said Charley; and making a lever of his right arm he raised Persse, and put him on his legs in a perpendicular position.

"That—that," said Persse, "has been done without violating in the slightest degree the recognized rules of grammar; per example—I rise, thou risest—"

Charley, without saying another word, placed his arm round that of Persse's as a retainer, and walked him off to the watchhouse.

"Your actions, sir," said Persse to Charley, "are those of a scholar, and if I mistake not are agreeable to the second rule in Syntax, which says that two or more nouns in the singular number joined together by one or more copulative conjunctions—your arm and mine, as in the present case, for instance—must have verbs, nouns and pronouns agreeing with them in the plural number—so that instead of *I* go, or *you* go, it is *we* go. You understand, don't you? I know you do."

"Yes, I understands you're a blamed fool," said Charley; and in a minute or two more Persse's name was on the books of the watchhouse.

"Persse," said the Recorder to him yesterday morning, "you were found lying on the banquette."

"Yes, may it please the court," said Persse, "I was

illustrating the neuter verb to lie."

"What business do you follow, Mr. Persse?" said the Recorder.

"I am a professor, sir, of the polite languages," said Persse.

"Your language was anything but polite in the watchhouse last night," said the Recorder.

"I may have been, thou mayest have been, he, she or it, at some period of their lives, may have been in a subjunctive mood, or represented under a *certain* condition," said Persse.

"I shall let you go this time," said the Recorder.

"*Verbum sat sapienti,* or as the vulgar translation has it, N. S." said Persse, and he left the office.

October 16, 1840

VI

*A New and
Improved Way
of Catching Fish*   PAT POWERS, George Smith
and John Ham, three youths
in their teens, did of their own
free will and accord, on Thursday the fifteenth of
October in the year of our Lord 1840, and the sixty-
fourth of our independence, individually and conjointly, agree, conclude and determine to go on a fishing party. Powers, who boasts of having been an imp
in a printing office, and consequently a youth of in-
telligence, was unanimously appointed a committee of

one to make preparations for the excursion. There was
only one question now open for discussion—whether
they should go in the broad day light, or when the
spirit of night shrouded land and water—whether Sol
or Cynthia should shine upon their amusements. Powers took the chair and put the question— Shall we go
on our fishing frolic by night? those in favor of the
motion will say, *aye,* those of a contrary opinion, *no.*
Smith said aye! Ham said no! it was a tye; but Powers
gave his casting vote in favor of going by night.

Bravo, bravo, chair, said Smith, and taking him by
the hand, he sung

> Day light may do for John Ham,
>   You know that he cannot well see,
> But there is something about the moon-man
>   That's delightful to you and to me.

Well it being fully understood that night was the time
fixed for their sport, about nine o'clock they all ren-
dezvoused on the levee. Powers had a skiff in waiting,
and they put out; he taking command.

"They toiled all night, but lo! they caught no fish."
What were they to do? Shade of Izaak Walton, were
they to return without a fish in their net bag? Powers
put the question, and they answered no, no, no! perish
the thought.

Well, they had only one place to supply themselves
from, and that was from the fish tanks lying in the

river at St. Mary's Market, in which the regular fish-
ermen had their supply for next morning's market
stored, with a view of keeping them fresh. They rowed
up to the tanks almost as silently as if their oars were
muffled, and having got there, commenced operations.
They had their bags full and were about to put out,
when one of the marine, or floating police of the second municipality very of-fish-ously bore up and made
them prisoners.

They were sent down to the calaboose for thirty
days each, where they will have an opportunity of re-
ceiving lessons from experienced masters in the art of
angling.

October 17, 1840

*Shifting the
Cargo*

THE victims having been all
dove-tailed into the dock, the
Recorder having seated him-
self on the bench, one policeman having called "order!" two or three others having instinctively echoed
"order," and the motley audience outside the bar having "shut up," and prepared themselves to pay due
attention to the proceedings of the court, the Recorder called "John French," and immediately a short
man, with a short neck and a short nose, answered
shortly, "Aye, aye, sir." French is a regular old iron-
sides of a fellow, with shoulders as broad as the keel
of a Dutch built vessel; there was a patch over each of

his sky-lights, as if he had been newly caulked, though his proboscis was any thing but ship-shape. The night was not sufficiently long to dissipate the effects of his dissipation, and when he rose to reply to the Recorder, he lurched on every side like a water-logged ship.

"French," said the Recorder, "you were found drunk last night."

French, through the agency of his tongue, caused his quid to revolve in his jaw—or in other words, like many of our present politicians, he made it change sides; he then gave a sudden jerk to his canvass trowsers, smoothed down with his dexter hand some stray hairs that grew on the deck of his head, and replied to the interrogatory of the judge:—

"Well, I b'lieves your honor, as how I was on a bit of a cruize."

Recorder.—What do you follow for a living?

French.—I follows the sea, your honor, and have done so, man and boy, for the last forty years; yes, your honor, Jack French has weathered many a gale —he has often been cast away on the lee shore of poverty, though he never saw a messmate yet raise the flag of distress, that he did not bear up to his aid and assist him, while a shot remained in the locker.

Recorder.—There were two bottles of whiskey found on your person—one in each pocket of your jacket.

French.—Why yes, commodore, you see as how I

was bent on a voyage, and I took on board a regular supply of sea store; them there two bottles of Monongahela [1] I stowed away in each of my pockets, by way of ballast, but may I be food for sharks if I could get along. I kept continually keeling over to the right; avast there, said I to myself, I don't set fair in the water, and with that, your honor, I took the bottle out that was to my starboard side, took a jolly good swig out of it, and put it back again.

Now thinks I, I guess I'll go right before the wind —no danger in putting out studding sails, but then, your honor, I found I lurched to the larboard side; I took out the bottle that was stowed away there and I lightened that, by anticipating my regular grog-time, and taking a hearty swig. Now, again I found myself inclining to the right, and I again took out the bottle. After having spun this yarn for your honor, you will see that I was doing no more than adjusting my ballast, when that piratical-looking craft there (pointing to the watchman) hauled me into port for the night. I only wish I was skipper over the lubber for one month, and if I wouldn't stop his grog may I never double Cape *Horn* again.

Jack having thus stated his case at length, he drew from his pocket a large piece of pigtail and replenished his quid. He hoped his honor would allow him to raise his anchor and put out to sea this time, and he assured

[1] A well-known whiskey of that time.

him that he would not be again caught water-logged in this port.

The Recorder assented, first giving him some wholesome advice that may serve him on future voyages. Jack paid dock fees, as he called the jail dues, and with a "heave a head my hearty!" he left the office.

August 19, 1840

The Schoolmaster Abroad

AMONG the droll customers who were up before Recorder Baldwin yesterday, Con O'Donnell was the drollest of the droll. Con is a book worm, a walking encyclopaedia of learned lore, a living edition of ancient and modern literature in one volume, a personification of the march of intellect, a moving model of the school master abroad. The different scars and cuts in his face represent an alphabet of Chinese hieroglyphics, and he looks himself like a badly bound, much-worn edition of the Connecticut blue laws.

Unfortunately for Con, he don't draw all his inspiration from the founts of literature; he too often quaffs libations of alcohol, and of the latter, as well as the former, he drinks deeply, believing that in both cases

> Shallow draughts intoxicate the brain,
> But drinking largely sobers men again.

When about to take a toddy, he closes his sinister optic, places it before his right one, looking at it as a *bon vivant* would at his first glass of favorite champagne, and commences conjugating it thus: "I love *thou*," &c., but if you ask him to decline it grammatically, he will tell you that it is a part of speech which is not to be declined at all—that although chemically speaking it is a liquid, yet in the orthographical sense of the term it is a substantive, and therefore not to be *declined*, but taken. After this learned explanation, he generally hides the toddy under his vest.

"O'Donnell," said the Recorder, "you are charged with being drunk last night."

O'Donnell—"*Difficilem oportet aurem habere ad crimina*, which means put not trust in the assertions of a Charley. There is no such word as drunk, may it please the court, known in the pure English vocabulary—it is one of those excrescences which have grown on our language, and in lopping off which with the axe of my intellect I am even now engaged."

"Drunk, sir," he continued, "is a vulgarism, a shaverism, or barberism as it is generally called—it is a bakerism, or to resort again to the vulgar, it is a loaferism. Instead of accusing me of being found drunk, if your honor had told me that I was in a state of mental hallucination, brought about by having imbibed certain inebriating potations, I could understand you; but when you speak of drunkenness to Con O'Donnell, you become perfectly unintelligible."

Recorder.—Term it what you will, you still seem to labor under its influence. Why is it that you so often get drunk?

O'Donnell.—Because, your honor, I adopt for my motto, *"dum vivimus vivamus,"* the free translation of which is, never to refuse a brandy toddy or gin cocktail when I can get it.

Recorder.—The watchman says that you were not only drunk, but that you acted like an insane person.

O'Donnell.—*Nil proprium ducas, quod mutari potest*—who is more like a mad man than one under the influence of inebriation.

Recorder.—Well, I shall let you go this time if you promise to keep sober.

O'Donnell.—I shall endeavor, may it please the court, but *haeret lateri lethalis arundo*, the deadly arrow (of intemperance) still sticks in my side—I cannot pluck it out.

Recorder.—Well, you may go and try the experiment—whereupon the door of the dock was opened by the policeman, and the learned Con O'Donnell withdrew.

August 21, 1840

CHARLEY GALLAGHER stood number one, if not in the good opinion of the court, at least on the prison list of the morning. Charley's head looked like a furze bush, his little gray eyes looked like two marbles in a toy shop, his potato masticators were like a white marble quarry; and, judging from appearances, he has as great an abhorrence of soap—not soft soap—as a tee-totaller has of alcohol.

"Charley Gallagher," said the Recorder.

"O faith thin, that's me purty self," says Charley, "and here I am, sure enough, quiet and comfortable as a pig at the ind of a praytee pit."

"Charley," said the Recorder, "you were arrested for disturbing the peace."

"Disturbing the payce!" says Charley, affecting astonishment; "why your anar, I might jist as well be accused of settin' fire to the Mississippy, or demolishing intirely the doom (dome) of the St. Charles Exchange; for purshumin to me, savin' the court's prisince, if I did ether one or the tother—not meself indade."

Recorder—"The policeman says you followed a woman into the watch-house, and would have assaulted and abused her but for his interference."

"O, Misther Baldwin," says Charley, giving an askance glance from the corner of his little eye at the Recorder—"that's a horse of a different color, altogether intirely, and as different from disturbin' the payce as a bog hole is from the river Shannon, or a shamrock from a cabbage lafe. If you jist listen I'll tell you all about that, while a piper 'ud be putting his bagpipes in tune. That was Biddy Flaherty, Mr. Baldwin."

"Was it?" said the Recorder, as if there *were* something in a name.

"It was, sur," says Charley, "and I'll tell you how it happened; as thrue as if it was comin' out of the mouth of the priest."

"Let us hear," said the Recorder.

Charley—Well you see, Biddy and I had a bit of private conversashun in the way of courtin' or the like, when sis she—

'Charley!' sis she.

'What's that, Biddy?' sis I.

'Why don't you make me a prisint,' sis she, 'as any body would that 'ud have a regard for a body,' sis she, jist that way.

'What'll you accept,' sis I—'a bonnit thrimmed with red ribbans or a parapleu?' *anglice* parasol.

'I'll take naither,' sis she, spaykin as stiff as if I was bound to playse her by act of parliament; 'if you want to show your love for me,' sis she, 'buy me a pair of Spanish leather shoes with bows in them.'

'Well, I'm contint, Biddy,' sis I; 'any thing at all for a quiet life, as the man sid whin he had the town bell rung to drown the noise of his wife's voice. But to make a long story short, your anar, I went and bought her the shoes, and that wouldn't do her but she should snap the change from a ten dollar bill I had in my hand, and that's what I was runnin' after her for; but I didn't disturb the payce at all at all.'

"Well," said the Recorder, "you have been up here before, so adopting your own language, to make a long story short, I shall send you to the calaboose, unless you find security to keep the peace."

So Charley was taken out, with liberty to take either horn of the dilemma.

August 22, 1840

*Statesmanship
Going to Waste*

TOM RODGERS, who has as many channels and seams and ravines in his face as there are in a twisted French loaf, claimed a legal right to a seat in Recorder Baldwin's court yesterday. From the story which the watchman told of Tom, he had been going the big figure on Friday night. He found fault with the Government for not having the Northeastern boundary question settled,[2] with the Florida army for not whipping the Indians,[3] and with the House of Representatives for refusing to admit the New Jersey

[2] The Northeastern Boundary, long a disturbing factor in the good relations of the United States and England, was finally settled two years later, in the Webster-Ashburton Treaty.

[3] The Seminole War had been going on for the past four years.

Whig members.[4] He spoke of the case of Lieutenant
Hooe, but whether he was in favor of, or against the
admission of the evidence of people of color, Charley
could not positively state. He thought hard cider very
good, particularly when diluted with brandy, and
thought it incumbent on the Government, but onerous
on the Whigs, to supply the people with log cabins.
He was in favor of an equal distribution of property,
and thought it the only way to annul the insidious
workings of the sub-treasury bill, as then every man
could be his own cash keeper. . . . So general were
his remarks, that the watchman would never have discovered his politics, but for the following few lines of
a song, which prove him to be a Whig—

> Cabbage grows in Kinderhook,
> And apples in North-bend,
> Harrison a soldier was—
> He's still a soldier's friend.

"Stop, stop," says Charley, who is *sub rosa* a Loco-
foco, "enough of that 'ere, I can't stand this here disturbing the peace no longer," and despite the en-
treaties of Mr. Rodgers he took him to the watch
house.

[4] Five Whigs contested the election of five Democrats in the New
Jersey delegation to the Twenty-Sixth Congress (March 4, 1839–
March 3, 1841), but finally lost on July 17, 1840.

The Recorder sent him down to the calaboose, to collect his ideas, for thirty days.

August 23, 1840

Luckless Dan THE mystical number of three formed the full number of prisoners who were up before Recorder Baldwin yesterday, and a trio of harder looking cases were never affected with the *rum*-atics.

The name of Dan Ingham took precedence of the other two. Alas for Dan! his life has been chequered with strange scenes. Now basking in the fitful sunshine of convivial enjoyment, and anon exposed to the clouds and the storms which follow dissipation. Dan's first or intemperate thoughts bespeak folly, frailty, mindless madness; his sober second thoughts, on the contrary, evince a well disciplined understanding, reflective faculties, and reasoning powers of a *high* order. Unfortunately for Dan, his first or intemperate thoughts almost perpetually occupy his mind, while the visits of his sober second thoughts are "few and far between." Hence the conclusion may be justly drawn that if Dan acts like a man of common sense sixty-five days in the year, during the other three hundred days he makes a regular *judy* of himself; or, to elucidate our subject by an arithmetical axiom, it will be seen that as 13 is to 62, so is the ratio of Dan's temperance to his propensity for liquor. We verily and religiously and most conscientiously believe that if there was not so much loaferism blended up with Dan's philosophy he would be somebody. Reader, did you ever see Dan? — "Himself alone's his parallel." He is of colossal proportions, somewhat like a walking windmill, his hands swinging about like a pair of the wings, his face is like the bark of a withered hickory tree, one of his optics is perpetually closed, his proboscis is like a patent powder horn, and his mouth looks like a large cavity in which provisions for a small army might be deposited.

"I find you are up here again, Mr. Ingham," said the Recorder.

Dan—(he was in possession of his sober second thoughts)—"Yes, Mr. Baldwin—

> It is my fate, my luckless lot,
> To ever seem what I am not;
> It is my destiny, I say,
> To come before you day by day,
> 'Til prejudice has put me down,
> A worthless loafer on the town;
> Your honor knows I am not so,
> Then why confine me—let me go!"

"Well," said the Recorder, "I will let you go this time, Dan, if you promise you will keep at your business and keep away from cabarets and watchmen."

Dan plighted his veracity that he would do as the court advised him.

The Recorder nodded to the police officer, which movement of his head acted like an *"open sesame"* on the door of the dock, and Dan walked out "jest as nat'ral!"

August 27, 1840

The Ubiquitous John Smith

THERE was but little business before Recorder Baldwin yesterday, and the consequence was that those who congregate outside the bar, with their mouths open and their coats off—who gaze upon the prisoners in the box with as much wonderment as if they were wild beasts in a menagerie—who laugh at the interrogations of the judge and the replies of the prisoners, although there may be nothing remarkably witty in either, and who, when the police officer cries "silence," endeavor to look as solemn as a mute at a funeral—the consequence was, we say, that these amateur admirers of criminal jurisprudence must have felt somewhat disappointed at the "lightness of the calendar."

John Smith—the never-stay-out-of-scrapes John Smith—the John Smith who appears to be possessed of the power of ubiquity, who is paddling his canoe on the western rivers, blasting rocks in St. Louis, fishing in Cape Cod, making shoes in Massachusetts, shearing sheep in Vermont, organizing a party of "hunters" on the Canadian line, crying clams in New York, engaged in a railroad riot in Philadelphia, drawing Fanny Elssler's carriage in Baltimore, making stump speeches against the Administration in North Carolina, a candidate on the Van Buren ticket in Illinois, a clock pedlar in Indiana, a steam doctor in Wisconsin, a "private correspondent" for the newspapers in Washington, the hero of a Bowie knife fight in Texas, a wounded prisoner of the Indians in Florida, an agent for the sale of Brandreth's pills in Georgia, a travelling preacher in Arkansas, a formidable "gouger" in Kentucky, a dealer in pork at Cincinnati, an agent of the Brandon Bank in Mississippi, an extensive cotton grower in Alabama, and a loafer in New Orleans at one and the same time. This omnipresent, ever-in-mischief, versatile, ever changing, always the same veritable John Smith was up yesterday before the Recorder.

"John Smith," said the Recorder.

"I'm here," said John, as quick as if he were a soldier expecting his rations.

"I think you have been up here before," said the Recorder.

"Never," said John, "I have followed the river all my life."

"Did I not see your name in a New York police report recently?" said the Recorder.

"Not a bit of it," said John—"never was north of Mason and Dixon's line in my life."

"Were you not a few days since charged with bigamy in Baltimore?" asked the Recorder.

"Impossible," said John; "how could I? I was never in the 'for better or worse' business but once in my life, and I have the marriage line here in my vest pocket to shew for that."

"Have you or have you not been connected with counterfeiters—passers of bad bills?" asked the Recorder.

"D—n clear of it," said John; "I'm altogether on the other side. I go in so strong for Benton mint-drops that I believe if I were to be de-*mint*-ed I could be coined into 'yellow boys.' "

"You have travelled a great deal through this country, have you not?" asked the Recorder.

"Only left home last evening; and I doubt if even now my anxious mother knows I'm out," said John.

The Recorder finding that there was not a loop-hole to be found in John's life on which to hang a charge, and that the one entered opposite his name in the watch returns of the morning was not a very venial one—merely kicking up a bit of a noise with one Thomas McSniffin, both of whom had been sniffing something more exciting than ice water—he discharged both of them on paying jail fees.

September 3, 1840

VII

THE solemn, emphatic and paternal admonition of Mr. Weller, senior, to his son was "bevare of vidders, Samivel, bevare of vidders." Now, although this counsel was specially intended for the guidance of his well beloved son, yet inasmuch as it was dictated by paternal affection and practical experience, its sincerity and wisdom are unquestionable; and it is therefore an injunction by a remembrance and observance of which the widow-admiring portion of mankind might keep out of scrapes and litigations innumerable. But widows, as well as gin toddies, have their devotees, and neither Parson Malthus, aided by Mr. Weller, nor Parson Matthew, aided by Mr.

Marshall, can wholly eradicate the predilection for both. But as the very high authority whose language we first quoted sagely remarked, we suppose "it's human natur," and can't be altered.

So much in the way of generalities, now for particulars. Yesterday Caroline Ohl, a Dutch widow, neither very fat nor very fair, but about forty, charged John Snabble, a young plump, good looking, red faced son of St. Nicholas with robbing her of $116.

Caroline, it appears, keeps a coffee house, and as John stood high in her favor she elevated him to the dignified and responsible office of head barkeeper. Being head barkeeper, he was going ahead as prosperously as he could have desired, and there seemed no bar to his future permanent happiness.

> To Caroline Ohl he'd sigh
> > And cry,
> O marry me, dear, or I'll die,
> > Ay, ay,
> Become Mrs. Snabble, *cut* all the Dutch rabble,
> > O my!
> Without a wherefore or a why.

The poetry and perseverance of Mr. Snabble was too much for the susceptible heart of the amiable Caroline to withstand, so that she became in everything but in name Mrs. Snabble, giving to him at the same time power over her goods and chattels, and control of all her domestic affairs: she even promised that ere the wane of many moons she would at the altar assume the poetical name of Snabble—Caroline Snabble!

But, alas, how mutable is worldly bliss, how unstable are worldly hopes! Mr. Snabble was not destined to enjoy for any lengthened time his enviable situation, or the smiles of the Widow Ohl. Jealousy, that poisonous ingredient, which never fails to turn the wine of love into the vinegar of hatred, wormed itself into the mind of the widow. From this moment the position of Mr. Snabble underwent a most extraordinary metamorphosis, and his path that was before strewed with odorous flowers now became covered with prickly thorns. Finding

> The venom clamors of a jealous woman,
> Poison more deadly than a mad dog's tooth,

he left her to fume and fret, and then put out for Natchez. After being there a short time he returned, and forgetting his present position—remembering only his previous one—he went to her box, as whilome was his wont, and took the money out of it in the best natured manner in the world, but which she accuses him of taking with evil intent.

The Recorder, after hearing an elaborate exposé of the facts and the merits of the case from the prisoner's counsel, Mr. Gaiennie, decided to send the case before the Criminal Court.

Oh! these vidders!

August 4, 1842

Trying to Influence the Judge

ELLEN SULLIVAN was found drunk and uproarious. "Well, Ellen, you're here again," said the Judge.

"Ah, yis, your honor," said Mrs. Sullivan, "but if ye'll jist be afther letting me go this time Ellen Sullivan is not the famale to throuble your honor agin."

"No, I shall not let you go; the calaboose is the best place for you."

"Ah, now, your swate honor, jist hear a poor widow whose husband's a hard working man. I own I took a small dhrop o' gin wid John Mahoney, to be sure, and it's meself that's sorry for that same. Plase to let me off now, your swate honor."

"No, I shall send you down for 30 days."

"Now I knows you be joking wid me; don't poke any of your nonsinse at Ellen Sullivan." And she gave the Recorder a knowing wink, at the same time dropping a courtesy.

But it was no go. Mrs. Sullivan was carried down, and this morning finds her an inmate of the Parish Prison.

June 27, 1840

*Determined to
Take the Oath*

Mrs. McCarty was found drunk. She was just out of the calaboose, and had sworn to her husband not to drink another drop for one year unless administered by his hand.

"I am sorry to see you here again, Mrs. McCarty," said the Recorder; "did you not swear that you would drink no more for one year?"

"Yes, your honor; but yesterday was Saint Patrick's day you know. But I'll make oath to it now," said Mrs. McCarty.

"Well, let me swear you," said his honor.

Mrs. McCarty approached and took hold of the book.

"You solemnly and sincerely swear," said the Recorder, "not to drink—"

"Yes, yes, your honor," said Mrs. McCarty, "unless my old man gives it to me."

"Hold, woman, I'll not allow you to add the sin of perjury to that of drunkenness," said the Judge, "you shall not swear at all."

"By Jasus," said Mrs. McCarty, "I *will* swear to that same," and seizing the book from the Recorder's hand, fell on her knees, and whilst the tears flowed freely from her eyes she swore, by the help of God, not to taste another drop, "until next St. Patrick's day."

She was discharged. Mrs. McCarty, take care to keep your oath.

March 19, 1840

Pity the Prisoner

LAST, though not least, in our report is Charley *Black* alias Brown; he was *blue* again!— Poor Charley, we fear, is a "gone sucker." He will get drunk and he will get into the watchhouse in spite of all we can say or do. We have no animosity against Charley; we dislike very much to put him in the police report, but we must do it. Perhaps he may reform when he reflects that his name is becoming conspicuous.—If we effect his reformation, if we save him from destruction, if we reclaim him from the "error of his ways," then shall our labor not have been in vain, and Charley will thank us for it.—The Recorder discharged him; and we hope never to be again compelled to record his name as unworthy of the Second Municipality.—Join the Temperance Society, Charley, and become a sober, decent man.

March 7, 1840

Dutch to the Judge

VICTOR SWAUGH was accused of threatening a man with personal violence. Victor can't speak one word of English; but he can talk Dutch like a book. He denied the charge made against him. Said he did not tell the man he would kill *him,* but that he was drunk and said he would kill *himself.*

"You plead not guilty, then, do you, Mr. Swaugh?" asked the Recorder.

"Yaw, mam, haw, jaw, law, vider stchriken schwipen hammer!!! Mynheer, schliden von struder, der schwitchen, die der swappenmatgen blutzer, gildenswipsey von derdeuch."

This was sufficient—no testimony was brought to disprove what Victor Swaugh said, and he was discharged.

June 30, 1840

Wise   GEORGE WISE made a d—n fool of himself by getting drunk and lying on the banquette in Poydras street. The watchman stirred him up, told him he was a watchman and no one else, and that he would take him to the watchhouse.

Wise—(*sings*)

> It's good to be merry and *Wise,*
>   It's good to be *corned* and *blue;*
> It's good to lie down when a feller is tired,
>   But it's bad to be taken by you.

"Brawo, brawo! that's a fact," says Charley; "you is sure of an endorsement for 30 days, and no mistake."

Charley was right in his anticipations; Wise got 30 days.

August 27, 1840

Royally Blue   MILES KING got royally blue, and was found in Poydras street, giving a lecture to a lamp-post on the science of government. He was discharged on paying jail fees.

August 12, 1840

Liquorised   JACOB BOND was found liquorised in Natchez street. As he could give no bond for his future good conduct, the Recorder ordered him thirty days in the calaboose.

August 12, 1840

Sacre   ROBERT LATHAM was found drunk in Girod st. He is an adulterated specimen of the genus loafer, and was about to be remanded until vouched for, when he claimed the hat which a fellow prisoner held in his hand.

"I want my hat which this man here has," said he. "Sacre!" said the man to whom he alluded—a little Frenchman with a snuffy colored face—"Sacre! you be one vera big rogue; this my chapeau."

The Recorder investigated the affair and found that

the Frenchman was right and that Latham was wrong, so he ordered him to be taken care of.

September 2, 1840

Whiskey-Taster MICHAEL FARRALL was accused of tapping whiskey barrels belonging to other people, and by means of a quill extracting the contents in sufficient quantities to satisfy his thirst for the 'crathur.' The Recorder thought this was cheating coffee-houses, and so gave Michael a ticket to the calaboose for 30 days, where he will be limited to a gill a day.

January 31, 1841

Long Out of the Calaboose CATHARINE LAKE, an old offender, was arrested in a "sink of iniquity" in Perdido street.

"How long since you came out of the calaboose, madam?" asked the Recorder.

"I have been out ever since last week," answered Catharine.

"Take her down, Mr. Constable," said the judge, and Catharine vanished to be locked up for one month.

July 29, 1840

Home in the Calaboose HENRY MCCANN, found used up on the levee.

Recorder—McCann, I think I have some knowledge of you.

McCann—I expect you have, Mr. Baldwin.

Recorder—Well, McCann, I'll send you down again.

McCann—How long this time, Mr. Baldwin?

Recorder—Ninety days, only.

McCann—Why, at this rate you'll never let me home to see my people.

He was taken down.

August 9, 1840

Poetry   JOHN HUGHES made a d—d fool of himself in Canal street, by playing the poet and holding converse with the moon. If there be any thing in this world to which a watchman has a deep and decided aversion, it is poetry; it matters not whether it be one of Moore's melodies or a hard cider song.[1] The consequence was, that John Hughes was taken peremptorialy to the watchhouse.

The Recorder sent him to the calaboose for thirty days, telling him he might turn his talent to "Prison Lyrics" in the meantime.

September 5, 1840

Self-Defense   WILLIAM DONNELLY, a descendant, we suppose, of the famous Dan Donnelly, the Irish pugilist, was arrested

[1] This, of course, refers to the songs of the Whig Party, which was at this time in the midst of its "log cabin, hard cider" campaign to elect William Henry Harrison president of the United States.

by the police in the act of giving practical and gratui-
tous lectures in the "noble art of self-defense" to a poor
fellow who cried "hold, enough!" without Donnelly's
paying any attention to the request. He was remanded
to find bail for his appearance at the Criminal Court.

September 9, 1840

Monongahela   MICHAEL CARROLL, arrested
on the wharf, as blue as Mo-
nongahela could make him, was sent down for thirty
days.

September 9, 1840

World Home   ROBERT GEORGE feeling the
whole country to be his inherit-
ance, has not burthened himself with the ownership
of any particular place of abode. He was found sleep-
ing under a wharf. The Recorder gave him a thirty-
days' ticket to the calaboose.

September 10, 1840